BRIGHTEST
OF
SILVER
LININGS

Climbing Carstensz Pyramid in Papua at Age 65

CAROL JEAN MASHETER PH.D.

Published by Aventine Press
55 East Emerson St.
Chula Vista CA 91911
www.aventinepress.com

ISBN: 978-1-59330-866-7

Library of Congress Control Number: 2014915867
Library of Congress Cataloging-in-Publication Data
Brightest of Silver Linings / Carol Jean Masheter, Ph.D.

Printed in the United States of America

In memory of Tendi Sherpa of Gudel VDC-4, Nepal, my climbing partner on Mt. Everest in May, 2008, who died in an avalanche on Mount Himlung in Nepal on September 29, 2013, at age 43 years. Rest in peace, Tendi Bai.

Acknowledgements

Many people helped to make this book possible as well as the experiences upon which it is based. I owe them deep gratitude. I would like to acknowledge at least a few of the many.

Thank you, Linda, for your tolerance of my passion for climbing mountains. I am blessed to have a sister like you.

Jason, I appreciate the knowledge you gained during your previous expeditions and your eagerness to share it. You shared valuable information, such as what we could expect in Papua and how to behave in unfamiliar and uncomfortable situations.

Dan, you took charge under difficult circumstances and led us capably. You fostered a cooperative spirit among strong personalities without being a dictator. I am grateful for your leadership and kindness.

Steven, I appreciate your quiet competence in managing local guides, your path finding through the jungle, and your familiarity with the climbing route. You kept us safe in an unsafe part of the world.

Jemmy, your skillful management of our volatile porters saved the day repeatedly. Thank you for reminding me to smile, especially when that was the last thing I wanted to do.

Raymond, your ready humor buoyed our spirits, and your creative cooking kept us well fueled. Good luck with finishing seminary and helping Papuans to live less difficult and more peaceful lives.

Dave, I am grateful for your friendship, humor, compassion, and dedication to supporting other team members, especially me. You inspire me to be a better person.

Pal, your patience and surrender of your accustomed leadership role for the sake of our team set a high standard for me to try to match. Thank you, too, for sharing your many fine photographs of our time in Papua.

Ivan, you have a special gift for connecting with local people and photographing their beauty and dignity. Thank you for your energy, honesty, and encouragement.

Denis, your quiet strength, courage, and determination inspired me believe in myself, when the going got tough. I respect your tenacious efforts to deal with the challenges of our jungle hike and the climb, as well as the capriciousness of the English language.

Dan, Dave, Pal, Ivan, and Denis, huge thanks for sharing your photographs, which are especially precious, as my camera stopped working before we got to the mountain.

Dale, Dori, Ben, Jeremy, Josh, and Nano, I enjoyed your curiosity and enthusiasm for adventure. Good luck with future family and individual explorations.

I am indebted to each of the Papuan porters from the Dani, Moni, and Dawa tribes for their invaluable help and many kindnesses. You taught me lessons in resourcefulness, compassion, and true generosity, which I will treasure always.

Carina, your positive energy helped me manage the frustration of repeated delays in Timika. Thank you.

Anna, your patience was awesome during our practice rock climbs. Alex, during our climb, I sometimes felt like a fool, but you never treated me like one. You both are awesome guides.

Thank you, John, for locating the only size small, 50-liter Gregory Alpinisto pack in North America and getting it to me before

I left for Papua. The pack performed admirably in challenging conditions. Its bright yellow color made me very visible both in the jungle and during the climb, which the guides appreciated.

I am especially grateful to all the readers who enjoyed my first book and encouraged me to write this one.

Addy, thank you for doing the kind of editing I requested. Your criticisms were fair and honest, exactly what I needed, even if I did not always want to hear them.

Table of Contents

Off My Rocker

I was furious. I paced in tight circles under a large gazebo near a cluster of posh shops and restaurants outside the gritty town of Timika in Papua, Indonesia. I had moved away from my companions to avoid spattering them with verbal acid. I had flown half way round the world at considerable expense to climb Carstensz Pyramid, a steep fin of limestone that rises to 16,000 feet elevation in mountainous jungle. After many delays and "guarantees" that failed to deliver, my companions and I had gotten nowhere near the mountain. The climb was over before it had begun.

I had heard that climbing Carstensz Pyramid could be challenging. Many things could go wrong and often did go wrong. However, lots of mountains are challenging. Take Mount Everest for example. Hundreds of people have died on Everest, since Sir Edmund Hillary and Tenzing Norgay summited it in 1953. Yet every year Everest lures hundreds more. As the highest mountain in the world, it has a certain cache, and many people have heard of it. Why, then, would anyone bother to climb a little-known, troublesome peak like Carstensz Pyramid? The short answer is the Seven Summits.

In the early 1980s a wealthy Texan businessman and amateur outdoorsman, Dick Bass, came up with the bold idea of climbing the highest peak in each of the seven continents, which he called the Seven Summits. However, some members of the mountaineering community have regarded the highest peak in Australia, Mount Kosciuszko at 7,310 feet elevation, as more of a hill than a mountain. The legendary mountaineer, Reinhold Messner, proposed that Carstensz Pyramid in Papua, Indonesia, a steep limestone fin of over 16,000 feet elevation, which he argued was the highest peak on the same tectonic plate as Australia, replace Mount Kosciuszko in the Bass list of the Seven Summits. In recent years increasing numbers of Seven Summiters have tried to climb the more challenging and inaccessible Carstensz Pyramid instead of Mount Kosciuszko. For additional details, please see the Appendix of this book and mountain guide Mike Hamill's recently published book, "Climbing the Seven Summits."

Why would a woman in her mid-60s who is afraid of heights risk life and limb to go to a troubled part of the world, like Papua, to climb a mountain? Why not stop with Mount Kosciuszko? Why climb at all? This book describes my reasons for wanting to climb Carstensz Pyramid, my preparation for the climb, the climb itself, and lessons learned along the way. It is based on entries in my travel journal as well as experiences as best as I can remember them. My companions may have experienced the same events and conditions differently.

I discuss some of the reasons for my involvement in high-altitude mountaineering in more detail in my first book, "No Magic Helicopter: An Aging Amazon's Climb of Everest." Briefly, when my life fell apart at age 50, I went to the Bolivian Andes for a break from the stress, loss, and anger I was experiencing. There I learned to climb and began to heal. I have learned some of the most powerful and valuable lessons of my life in the mountains.

One climb led to another. At age 60, I climbed Aconcagua, the highest peak in South America and my first of the Seven Summits. I had no plans to climb the entire list at that time, but the idea of climbing the highest peak in the Western Hemisphere intrigued me. Then I climbed Kilimanjaro as a test of a new fitness program I was using to prepare for trying Everest. Summiting Everest six months later was the happiest day of my life. When I returned home, a local TV reporter asked me, "You don't look like the kind of woman who would be content to sit in your rocker. What's next?" I mumbled something about the Seven Summits, more to have some kind of answer than out of real commitment. I was thin, tired, injured, and still getting my head around the fact I had summited Everest at age 61 and had survived. I thought I was done with climbing big mountains.

About three months later, after I had recovered from Everest, a strong urge to climb returned. I thought, *why not try the rest of the Seven Summits?* Denali in Alaska and Mount Elbrus in Russia followed. Three months after turning 65 years of age, I stood on the summit of Vinson Massif in Antarctica, my sixth of the Seven Summits. Only one more remained. I asked myself, *would it be Mount Kosciuszko or Carstensz Pyramid?*

What I had heard about Carstensz Pyramid both intrigued and frightened me. Certainly Mount Kosciuszko would be safer and cheaper. I was concerned about recent violence in Papua, the rigors of several days of strenuous hiking through mountainous jungle to reach Carstensz Pyramid, and the steep climb to its summit. However, I was not sure I would be content with finishing my Seven Summits with a hill instead of a mountain. Besides, since childhood, jungles have fascinated me. During my 20s, I signed up for a trip down a remote part of the Tana River in Kenya in dugout canoes. I imagined a Tarzan jungle with tropical trees and flowers, exotic birds, and chattering monkeys swinging through the forest canopy. However, the trip was cancelled. Maybe now, over 40 years later, was my chance to fulfill a longstanding dream to experience a jungle. Also, I am not proud of this, but I did not want others to say, "She couldn't do Carstensz Pyramid, because it was too hard for a 65-year-old woman." I decided to go for it.

In spite of its scary reputation, expeditions to climb Carstensz Pyramid tended to fill quickly. In the fall of 2011 I contacted Adventure Consultants, the mountain guide company with which I had summited several of the Seven Summits. This company's guides had been supportive of me as an older female mountaineer. They knew me, and I trusted them.

I applied for a place on their expedition to climb Carstensz Pyramid in March, 2012. Applying for such a climb with a reputable mountain guide company is a bit like applying for a job. Applicants send their climbing resume, listing which climbs they have done with which guides. The purpose of the application is to screen applicants for appropriate skills, experience, and fitness level, so each applicant is an asset rather than a liability to the expedition.

Though I had climbed with Adventure Consultants before, I was nervous about whether they would accept me for this particular climb. A couple weeks later, notification of my acceptance arrived. I floated in a happy cloud of relief and anticipation, as I signed a contract and paid the expedition cost of 18,500 U.S. dollars (USD), which included climbing permits, payment for mountain guides and porters, transportation costs and some lodging expenses within Papua, food and cooking fuel for the hike through the jungle, and other local expenses. I was in!

In late January, 2012, I had returned from a wonderful climb of Vinson Massif in Antarctica. After a few days to recover from a cold I had caught near the end of that trip, I began to prepare for Carstensz Pyramid. With just five weeks before my departure for Papua, my preparation began with reviewing the Adventure Consultants gear list for the Carstensz Pyramid expedition. My gear for previous climbs was designed for very cold, dry conditions: a down sleeping bag rated to minus 25 degrees Fahrenheit for Everest Base Camp, a second down sleeping bag rated to minus 40 degrees Fahrenheit for the camps above Base Camp and which I had used for Denali, Mount Elbrus, and Vinson Massif, a thick down parka and huge down pants that made me look and feel like a stuffed toy, and bulky, three-layer Millet mountain boots.

Most of this gear would not be suitable for the hot, humid jungle hike to and from the peak and a very long day of climbing, possibly in freezing rain and snow. The Carstensz Pyramid gear list specified a synthetic-filled sleeping bag rated to 15 degrees Fahrenheit rather than a down sleeping bag. I already owned several down bags. I was reluctant to purchase yet another bag with my dwindling funds, but I understood Adventure Consultants' reasoning. When down gets wet, it loses its ability to keep a sleeper warm. Once wet, down is difficult to dry, especially in wet and humid conditions. Carstensz Pyramid was located in a jungle with daily rains year round. I found a synthetic-filled sleeping bag rated to 15 degrees Fahrenheit at Backcountry.com and bought it.

For clothing, I had suitable, lighter weight base layers and mountain boots, but I needed thinner climbing pants, jackets, and gloves. The equipment list also included two complete rain suits, the reasoning being that thorns in the jungle and the sharp limestone of the climb would shred our rain gear. I sold some of my old mountaineering gear and found most of what I needed at my favorite local climbing shop, IME in Salt Lake City. Polly Wiessner, an anthropologist acquaintance, who has done field work in Papua New Guinea, recommended Edgewater's knee-high, insulated mud boots for the hike through the jungle, so I bought a pair online.

For my fitness program, I gradually increased my workouts to promote strength and endurance. At a local gym, I worked with free weights and did pull ups to strengthen my upper body. I used resistance machines to strengthen my abdominal muscles and legs. For endurance, I gradually increased the speed and distance of my runs. For the summit climb, I went to a climbing gym and practiced, first in rock shoes, then in the boots I planned to use on summit day, my La Sportiva Evo Nepal mountain boots. I took yoga classes for flexibility, balance, and core strength. I continued to ride my mountain bike around town, when the winter roads were not too icy. When the avalanche risk was not too high, I snowshoed and backcountry skied in the nearby Wasatch Mountains for longer training sessions. All was going according to plan.

I looked for flights from Salt Lake City to Denpasar, Bali, where I would meet the guides and the other team members. Using the Internet, I tried to find cheap round trip airfare. Even the fares on websites, like Travelocity and Expedia, were very expensive. I tried contacting travel agents who had helped me in the past, but they did not return my emails. I tried the Internet again, finally found a good buy, and bought my plane tickets on February 1. Pleased with myself, I checked off that task from my to-do list.

The day after I had paid for my airline tickets, Adventure Consultants emailed me. They wanted an additional 2,000 USD for the Carstensz Pyramid trip. Also, they had changed the expedition meeting place from Denpasar, Bali, to Timika, Papua, which would cost me at least another 1,200 USD in additional air travel. Perhaps some of the other expedition members had dropped out, so Adventure Consultants needed more money from the rest of us in order to run the trip. However, I did not have the additional 3,200 USD. I had retired from my last profession on January 1, 2012, in order to climb Vinson Massif and then Carstensz Pyramid. I had paid for both climbs, while I was still working. As a new retiree, my retirement income had not started. I was living off financial fumes.

I asked Adventure Consultants for other options. Very graciously, they mentioned that Mountain Trip, a company based in Ophir, Colorado, was also running a Carstensz Pyramid climb in early March, 2012. I had not heard of Mountain Trip, so I Googled them. Bill Allen, one of the company's owners, had run six Carstensz Pyramid trips in recent years. On five of those trips, expedition members had summited. Their safety record looked OK. Their Carstensz Pyramid trip was shorter than Adventure Consultants', 14 instead of 17 days, but the price was the same. Mountain Trip's expedition cost included the flight from Denpasar to Timika as well as helicopter access to the base of the actual climb, avoiding the strenuous jungle hike.

I was surprised. Several other mountain guide companies had provided helicopter access recently, but they now claimed that such access was unreliable, and they no longer offered it. A few other climbers I knew had hired drivers to take them through the Freeport Mine. However, access to the Mine road has been controlled by a complex and unreliable web of influence. A guide friend of mine tried to sneak through the Mine a decade ago, was caught, and held prisoner in a large metal container. He escaped, was recaptured, and eventually had to pay a substantial bribe for his freedom. Driving through the Mine did not seem to be any safer or more reliable than helicopter access.

For the next few days I weighed the pros and cons of Mountain Trip's Carstensz Pyramid expedition. Part of me balked at the helicopter option. I had psyched myself up for Adventure Consultant's jungle hike. I had already bought special mud boots and had been training for the hike. Flying in a helicopter from Timika at sea level to Base Camp at nearly 14,000 feet elevation would not provide the gradual acclimatization of walking several days through the jungle to Base Camp. Climbing another 2,000 vertical feet within a day or two after arriving at Base Camp would be at best very strenuous and at worst put members of our team at risk for altitude sickness. Also, daily rain storms and rugged terrain made flying dangerous, especially for helicopters.

On the other hand, flying by helicopter was seductive. The flight to Base Camp would avoid rumored dangers of the jungle hike -- the possibility of being kidnapped by tribal warriors, porters going on strike and abandoning us, being injured or becoming ill in the jungle, to name a few. Also, the jungle hike to Carstensz Pyramid Base Camp sounded really strenuous. Maybe I had done enough strenuous things in my life. *Now that I was nearing age 66, there was no shame in taking the easier way to the mountain,* I told myself and my friends. Besides, I had never flown in a helicopter and wanted to see what it would be like.

The positive aspects of the Mountain Trip expedition outweighed my concerns. A few days after I sent my application for their Carstensz Pyramid climb, Mountain Trip accepted me. Adventure Consultants graciously transferred what I had paid them to Mountain Trip. Frustration and anxiety shifted to happy relief. I was back on track to climb Carstensz Pyramid.

Within a few days Mountain Trip sent me a list of names and email addresses of the guide and two other client climbers. Mountain Trip suggested that we contact each other and tell a little about ourselves. This seemed like a good idea. I composed a short email, hoping I sounded friendly and competent but not too cocky. I pictured the guide and the other climbers as being leaner and younger than myself. I hoped I would be able to keep up with them. Kevin Koprek, our expedition leader, and Carina Raiha (pronounced KahREENa RYEya), the other woman climber on the trip, each sent friendly replies. I received no reply from the other climber, Dennis Uhlir. *Perhaps he is busy getting ready for the trip,* I told myself, but I felt a little rejected.

I looked up each of the team members on the Internet. Kevin had experience with high-angle rescues, skills I found reassuring for our steep climb. Carina was the first Norwegian woman to summit Everest. Dennis had summited Everest recently with Adventure Consultants. I looked forward to meeting them and sharing our Everest experiences. Our guide and my fellow climbers seemed well qualified to climb Carstensz Pyramid.

A couple of weeks later the Mountain Trip staff asked whether I wanted to share a hotel room in Bali and Timika with a newly added, fourth member of our team, whom they described as a young man from Malaysia. Sharing a room with a stranger sometimes works, but it sometimes does not. If he had different expectations than mine about what sharing a room meant, that could be awkward. Since I had not yet met him, I decided against it. I scraped together another 400 USD and paid Mountain Trip for a single supplement, so I could have my own hotel room.

As departure day approached, emails from Mountain Trip changed in tone. While they still seemed confident that they could provide helicopter access, they advised us to come prepared for the jungle hike as Plan B. *Fine,* I thought. I had been running, bicycling, snowshoeing, and hiking in preparation for the possible jungle hike. I already had knee-high mud boots. I would bring them in case we went with Plan B.

March 1, 2012. Today was the day before departure day. My former colleague, Tom Hudachko, had released a news advisory about my goal to become the oldest woman in the world to climb the Seven Summits. Tom had suggested that I be available for interviews from 4 to 5 p.m. at my home today. I was not sure what to expect, but I tidied up the usual chaos that takes over my house, when I am packing for a foreign trip. Just before 4 p.m. a reporter with a scraggly, gray pony tail and big belly showed up. He asked me to sit in my rocking chair, something I never do, while he asked me questions and videotaped my answers. He had me hold up some of my climbing gear and a copy of my first book for the camera.

In contrast to my previous encounters with reporters, this guy seemed uninterested and just going through the motions. I told myself, *one bored reporter is better than no reporters.* I compensated for his low energy by answering his questions with extra enthusiasm. *At least I'm having a good time,* I tried to convince myself, but in fact I felt awkward and a bit silly. *This is the unglamorous side of being "a little bit famous,"* I thought wryly.

Enchanting Bali

March 4, 2012. After three days of long flights and layovers in airports, I arrived at the airport in Denpasar, Bali, my first trip here. My expectation to spend a few relaxing days exploring the Denpasar area was shattered. My checked luggage, two duffels of mountain gear, did not arrive in the baggage claim area. My gut twisted in panic. Trying to find replacement mountain gear would be impossible in a city known for its tropical beach holidays. I reminded myself, *the best remedy for panic is to take positive action.* I looked for the desk to report missing baggage.

Lots of other passengers also were missing luggage. Instead of a queue, they formed an irritable mass several people deep around the complaint desk. Finding the appropriate forms and describing my missing duffels took a long time. I struggled to describe the colors of my duffels, bronze and purple, to an official whose understanding seemed to be limited to the colors, blue, red, and black. The rest of the members for the climbing expedition were not due to arrive for a few more days. *My duffels could still show up, before we leave Denpasar for Timika,* I tried to reassure myself.

Certain that my airport contact person would have left by now, I steeled myself to find an honest taxi driver, a task I had found daunting on previous trips to unfamiliar cities. I shouldered my climbing pack and wove through the crowds to the airport terminal exit. On my way I found a currency exchange booth and exchanged 10 USD for about 100,000 Indonesian Rupiah (100,000 R), hoping it would be enough for the taxi to the Sanur Beach Hotel, where I had made online reservations before leaving home and would meet the rest of the expedition members in a few days.

Near the exit from the airport terminal I spotted a slender little man in a sarong, holding a sign with my name. I smiled with relief. The driver greeted me, "hello, madam, how you?" I thanked him for waiting for me, while I had been dealing with my missing duffels. My Indonesian was limited to a few basic words, so I was glad that he spoke some English.

I settled myself and my climbing pack in the back seat of the taxi and tried to fasten the seat belt. It didn't work. *I must trust the local deities,* I thought wryly. Traffic was very heavy, slowing our progress to a crawl, which lowered the risk of a high speed crash and gave me opportunities to take in the sights. The novelty of seeing Bali for the first time helped counteract jetlag and worry about my missing mountain gear.

The afternoon sky was thick with low clouds, the air heavy with humidity from recent rain. Narrow, muddy side roads branched off haphazardly from our paved street, merchant's stalls jammed together almost on top of each other, and crowds of pedestrians tried to avoid dirty puddles. Bougainvillea vines, spangled with orange and purple flowers, spilled over walls dark with moss. Large, white magnolia blossoms shone against thick clusters of large leaves, so dark they were nearly black. Elaborate stone statues of deities and demons leered from entrances to gated court yards. Over some of the side roads, long bamboo poles arched gracefully, each ending with a mysterious pendant. Denpasar seemed to be a crazy quilt of the elegant, the mysterious, and the shabby.

Swarms of motorbikes darted among SUVs, mini-buses, and taxis. Slender Balinese men bent over their motorbikes like race-horse jockeys and wove through traffic with brazen abandon. Sometimes a woman in a bright sarong sat behind a motorbike driver, sometimes with one or two little kids behind her. Most of the motorbike drivers wore flashy helmets, but few of the women and none of the children did. One little girl dressed all in white – white dress, white hat, white stockings, white shoes -- sat side saddle, serene and spotless, behind her driver, while he drove the motorbike around muddy potholes.

I stared around in wonder, feeling like a stranger in a strange land. I wished I knew more about what I was seeing. I asked my taxi driver, but we had few words in common. Trying to converse overtaxed my jetlagged brain. We settled into silence, while he negotiated the complex currents of traffic. It took an hour to cover the seven miles from the airport to the hotel.

Behind a high wall of moldy stucco and down a narrow drive, the Sanur Beach Hotel was an island of luxury. The spacious lobby was tastefully decorated with Balinese wall art, sculpture, and blooming moth orchids. A few plump European tourists wearing shorts strolled by. Slender Balinese men wearing matching sarongs and head bands greeted me with a graceful "Namaste" and a little glass of very tasty, yellow fruit juice. I settled into my room on the fourth floor with the modern conveniences that foreign tourists expect: tastefully modern décor, private bath with modern plumbing, king-size bed, wide-screen TV, air conditioning, clean sheets and towels.

In spite of my long flights and little sleep, I did not feel tired, so I went outside to explore. It was early evening. The Equatorial heat did not feel as oppressive as it had at the airport. Stone paths wound through the hotel's spacious grounds past swim pools, tropical trees, and exotic statues. Flowers I remembered from my childhood in Southern California bloomed everywhere: hibiscus, fuchsia, bougainvillea, calla lilies. Frangi pangi scented the air with heavenly fragrance. Fallen blossoms laced the walkways like perfect, white stars. Doves with stylish spotted dickeys cooed in the trees. Someone, perhaps a devout staff member, had tucked fresh, pink hibiscus flowers behind the ears of the stone demons and clothed them with sarongs of dark green and white plaid. I had stepped into a culture very different from my own. Unable to understand the significance of what I was seeing, I felt as ignorant and naïve as a very young child.

March 7, 2012. The day after I arrived in Denpasar I had taken a taxi through traffic-jammed streets back to the airport and spent long, hot hours recovering my missing duffels. Though the process was slow and inefficient, all my mountain gear was present and intact. Relieved, the next few days had felt like a mini vacation at a luxury spa, while I waited for the guide and other expedition members to arrive. I had taken a yoga class in a raised bamboo shelter on the beach, played tag with the lazy, little waves that lapped the nearby sand, looked for sea shells among washed up seaweed and garbage, wondered about mysterious little offerings of flowers, sweets, and coins I found in the morning on the beach and in shop doorways, gone for a bike ride with a local guide and visited a school full of energetic little boys eager to practice their English on me, had a Balinese massage, and had my feet bathed in a basin of floating flower pedals.

The Sanur Beach Hotel's breakfast buffet was a lavish spread that spanned European and Asian cuisines: eggs, sausage, bacon, potatoes, pastries, hot and cold cereals, local Balinese and Indonesian dishes of rice or noodles with vegetables and chunks of spicy, fried chicken, and wonderful fresh fruits and juices: papaya, pineapple, green melon, and mango. I filled a plate with fruit, yogurt, two tiny beef sausages, and a miniature chocolate-filled croissant, a sharp contrast with my usual Spartan breakfast at home – oatmeal with non-fat milk and a sliced banana. I carried my breakfast to a small table on the edge of the dining patio. The air was so thick and heavy with humidity, dew drops grew miraculously before my eyes at the tip of each blade of wheat grass in a tiny living arrangement on my table. I had never witnessed this before. I watched, fascinated.

The languid beauty of Bali had been exotic and enjoyable, but I was ready for the next phase of this trip, the reason I had come here, to climb Carstensz Pyramid. I was eager to meet the mountain guide and my fellow climbers, who were scheduled to arrive today. A lean Western man a bit taller than me, perhaps in his 30s, walked past my table. He carried a messenger bag and wore a crumpled, short-sleeved shirt, cargo shorts, and sandals. He looked like a mountain guide. I went over to introduce myself.

"Would you be Kevin Koprek with Mountain Trip?" I asked. He looked up, grinned broadly, and replied, "Would you be Carol?" We both laughed. He offered me the chair opposite him at his table.

Over breakfast, I jabbered about my previous climbs. Kevin listened politely. I was talking too much, I realized, perhaps because I wanted to convince Kevin that I was qualified for this climb in spite of my age. Trying to balance the conversation, I asked Kevin about himself. He replied that he was interested in how people make crucial decisions under pressure, such as during rescues. When I asked him what he liked about being a mountain guide, he replied that he liked meeting new people and teaching them mountain skills. Kevin impressed me as a smart, well-qualified guide as well as a likeable man. After breakfast we both had errands to run, so we parted ways, until our first team meeting scheduled for noon.

As I passed through the hotel lobby, a sturdy woman in her 40s with short blond hair asked whether I was with Mountain Trip. She introduced herself as Carina, one of the expedition members, who had responded to my email a few weeks ago. Carina was talkative and glowed with happy energy. She introduced Mika (pronounced MEEka), a quiet, good-looking man with a shaved head. Mika had a pleasant gaze and the smooth, muscled physique of a guy who worked out at a gym regularly. Carina and Mika had recently married, no doubt one reason she was so upbeat. Mika was not a member of our team. He would explore Bali on his own, while we climbed. He and Carina would then vacation together afterwards. As we chatted in the lobby, Carina did most of the talking. I tried to include Mika, but he seemed content to stay quietly in the background.

At noon, Kevin told Carina and me that Dennis had been delayed and had not arrived yet. Kevin had not heard anything from Qobin (pronounced KObin), our fourth group member. Our first team meeting would be postponed, until after they arrived. We were scheduled to leave the hotel tonight to fly to Timika. My gut tightened. Delays so early in our trip could snowball, potentially ending this climb before it could even begin.

Dennis and Qobin did arrive later in the day. We were back on track. My gut relaxed. Our first team meeting followed a familiar pattern. We introduced ourselves and said a little about our past climbing experiences. Dennis was in his 40s, stocky with dark hair and light eyes, and a bright smile. He was originally from the United States but was now living in London. Like Carina, he had been a corporate lawyer. Qobin had a broad face, tilted eyes, meaty shoulders, and a big belly. Thirty years of age, he worked for an influential politician in Malaysia's government. He had summited Everest in 2004. Neither Dennis nor Qobin looked very fit, but first impressions had fooled me before. Perhaps they wondered whether I was too old for this climb. I reminded myself, *each of us had summited Everest. We each are working on completing the Seven Summits. These are good indicators of each team member's commitment to this climb.*

Kevin gave us an overview of our expedition. On summit day we each would have a radio, so we would be able communicate with each other and descend from the summit at our own pace. During my descent from Everest's summit in 2008, I had gone completely blind. I had repeatedly asked my two Sherpa climbing partners to radio our expedition leader and explain the situation – why I was taking so much time to descend. For some reason, they never radioed him. After that terrifying experience, I really liked the idea of having my own radio.

All the team members and climbing gear had arrived in Denpasar. Tonight we would fly to Timika as planned. We were making progress now. I felt happy and optimistic. In the meantime, we had last-minute preparations for our red-eye flight tonight. Qobin and Dennis stayed at the hotel to repack, while Kevin and I decided to go for a walk and look for a restaurant we both liked. The day's fierce heat had softened to velvety warmth, so our stroll through crowds of tourists and locals was pleasant. We scanned several daily menus chalked on blackboards before agreeing on a modest place with outdoor seating. A light supper of stir-fried chicken and vegetables followed by a dab of chocolate ice cream under a patio umbrella was perfect as a pre-flight meal. Kevin graciously picked up our bill.

Mountain Trip's local operator, Franky Kowaas, a stocky Indonesian in his 40s, met us at the airport before midnight. Franky energetically helped us find baggage carts, get plane tickets, check bags, pass through security, and get all the necessary stamps, stickers, and seals. His energy helped me shake off a strong undertow of sleepiness, as midnight came and went.

In the wee hours we settled into our plane seats. I had a window seat, as I preferred. Dennis had the aisle seat in the same row. When we had met earlier today, he had seemed carefree and friendly. Now he was quiet, even sullen. Soon after our plane took off, he got up abruptly and found another seat. I wondered whether I had offended him somehow. I tried not to dwell on it. Maybe he was just tired from his delayed flight to Denpasar and wanted to be alone. Happy to be on our way, I grinned at a slender, middle-aged Indonesian man across the aisle. He grinned back. It felt good to be on our way to Papua.

Helicopter Tomorrow

March 8, 2012. The three-hour flight went more quickly than I had expected. As the sky lightened, our plane descended, slicing through a layer of gray clouds. Below us I could see an expanse of dark green trees dotted with white clouds, then cleared fields, scattered huts, a town, and then a paved runway.

After landing we deplaned onto the runway and got onto buses that would drive us to the airport terminal. Carina and I moved down a crowded aisle toward a couple of empty seats near a guy with straw-blond hair and a very weathered face. He was wearing ostrich-skin cowboy boots. Carina asked him whether he was with the Freeport Mine. He said yes. Excited about our own adventure, I volunteered that we were here to climb Carstensz Pyramid. Cowboy Boots frowned, shook his head, and said grimly, "You're looking for trouble. There have been recent killings." I almost said, *I don't want to hear this,* but I kept quiet. Cowboy Boots continued with vague warnings about unspecified dangers, between muttering into two Smart Phones, one in each hand.

In the crowded baggage claim area, we waited along a worn conveyor belt for our duffels. Cowboy Boots rushed around, popping up like a jack-in-the-box above the crowd, taking pictures of each member of our team. His picture-taking had a grim intensity to it, like he was on a special mission. Kevin sidled up to each of us and said quietly, "Be low key, don't tell anyone we are here to climb Carstensz Pyramid." *Now you tell us,* I thought sourly. *Had I known that, I would not have said anything to Cowboy Boots about our climb.*

Trying to put this weirdness out of mind, I spotted my duffels and heaved them onto a baggage trolley. Everyone else found their bags, plus several Mountain Trip duffels of group equipment. We guided our loaded trolleys through the crowd, followed Franky through customs, and piled our duffels and ourselves into a dark SUV with tinted windows.

As the sun rose above the trees, our driver, Remmy, a slender, young Indonesian man wearing designer jeans, drove us from the airport into town. In contrast to the shabby glamour of Denpasar, Timika's roads and shops looked grimy and cheerless even in the clean early morning light. Rubbish spilled into the streets and clogged muddy rivers. Pedestrians sluggishly picked their way over broken concrete and around piles of garbage along the roadside. A few people scowled at our SUV, as we drove through swarms of motor bikers and beat-up micro-buses jammed full of local people. This was no resort town.

Our drivers pulled into a tiny, walled courtyard. A uniformed guard swung a single rusty rail behind our SUV, presumably to protect us, from whom or what I was not sure. We had arrived at the Grand Tembaga, the hotel where we would stay, until we flew to Base Camp. I got out of the SUV and stared. The hotel was a crazy mixture of kitsch and dignity. It was painted a whimsical shade of what could be best described as orange-sicle, yet it had a gracefully curved portico and stately white pillars flanking an arched entrance. The Grand Tembaga, I later learned, was the best hotel in town, favored by airline crews and journalists. The lobby was air-conditioned, a dealmaker for me in Timika's heat, which felt even more oppressive than Denpasar's.

The Grand Tembaga had only four rooms for the five of us. I had prepaid an extra 400 USD for a private room. Apparently everyone else also expected their own room. None of the guys would share with each other. Carina invited me to share with her. I felt just as entitled as the guys to a private room and preferred a room of my own, but I agreed to share in the spirit of being a good team player. I had learned on previous climbing trips that private rooms were not always available, even after I had prepaid for one.

After we each had moved our bags into our rooms, we met in the dining room behind the lobby for a buffet breakfast. Its offerings did not match the lavish variety of the Sanur Beach Hotel, but the chunks of fried chicken in spicy sauce and the fresh mango juice were good.

Over breakfast Kevin told us that our helicopter needed routine maintenance, which would take three weeks. *Three weeks! Our entire trip was only two weeks long! How did this happen?* I wondered. Kevin and Franky said they were talking with another helicopter company. One thing was certain. We would not fly today. After our team meeting, I exercised to keep in shape for our climb and to dissipate frustration about the delay. I climbed up and down the hotel stairs and did "burpees," as Kevin had showed me. For each burpee, I stood tall, bent over and touched my toes, squatted, jumped my feet back to high plank position, did a push up, jumped my feet to my hands, and jumped up into the air. Then Carina and I paddled around in the little swim pool in the hotel's courtyard to beat the intense afternoon heat.

March 9, 2012. Over last night's dinner, Kevin had told us the second company's helicopter had a rotor problem. This morning at breakfast, Franky had told us that he had talked to a third helicopter company. Their pilot was sick. Maybe we could fly on March 13 or 14. Maybe we could fly later today or tomorrow. I knew that such delays and uncertainties were common in this part of the world, but a sense of uneasiness began to grow. One thing was clear. We would not fly today.

Kevin had advised us not to leave the hotel. If we did leave, he had suggested that we not wear bright colors, cover our arms and legs in deference to local dress customs, and avoid attracting attention to ourselves. Kevin's warnings made me uneasy. I dreaded facing the heat outside the hotel, but I did not like the idea of being cooped up all day. Carina and I needed to buy bottled water. We could buy it at the hotel, but the bottles it sold were small and expensive. During my previous travels, I had learned that prices were usually better at shops or stalls outside hotels. Carina and I asked the guys whether they wanted to go with us. Qobin was hunched over his laptop and barely looked up. Dennis seemed even less motivated. Carina and I decided we would go on our own.

Outside the hotel's air-conditioned lobby, the late-morning heat hit me like a wall, leaving me feeling dull and unmotivated. I wished I had worn shorts like Carina instead of my white, long-sleeved shirt and tan, zip-leg, hiking pants. Our first challenge was to cross the street to the nearest shops. The wide thoroughfare surged with speeding motorbikes, taxis, and mini-buses. The traffic had no predictable pattern or lanes. Drivers ignored the one stop light just up the road from the hotel. *They probably would not think twice about running over a couple of foreign women,* I thought grimly. *We would need to be nimble and quick.*

When a small gap in the traffic appeared, I ran, weaving among speeding vehicles across the street toward Tops, the nearest thing to a grocery store we could see. Now pulsing with adrenalin and beaded with sweat, I paused and looked back to be sure Carina was OK. She was strolling through the currents of traffic, apparently unconcerned. I had to smile at the contrast between her relaxed saunter and my tightly wound energy. At least my sprint had shaken off my lethargy. Inside Tops we wandered through its aisles, until we found bottled water. We paid a tiny young cashier wearing a black Islamic head covering. She ducked her head and avoided looking at us. I wondered whether she found us to be exotic, weird, interesting, scary, indecent, or something else.

Already wilted by the heat, I wanted to return to the hotel and cool off in the little swim pool. Carina wanted to explore further. I followed reluctantly. We picked our way along the main thoroughfare. In places we skirted high walls bordering the roadside to avoid being hit by speeding motorbikes and mini-buses. We stepped over chunks of broken pavement strewn with trash and around puddles of muddy water. The acrid stench of rotting garbage mixed with hot dust stung my nostrils. We passed dark sheds, inside which we could make out piles of plump sacks, probably fifty-pound bags of rice. Near a jumble of closely parked motorbikes, a simple set of shelves displayed plastic water bottles refilled with gasoline, the closest thing to a gas station I had seen here. On muddy corners a few dark Papuan men and women with deep-set eyes and very short, kinky hair had spread faded cloths and sat behind little piles of local fruits and imported packaged snacks, apparently hoping to make an occasional sale.

In contrast to the dire warnings from Cowboy Boots at the airport and Kevin at our team meetings in the hotel, people either ignored us or were friendly. Several young Indonesian guys on motorbikes stopped to practice their English with us. A few asked us to take their pictures. They grinned, struck bold macho poses for our cameras, and then sped off, waving at us merrily.

As we walked down a dirt side road, local children followed us. Carina was especially good at engaging them. A slender little boy in bright yellow shorts spontaneously danced for us. A little girl sitting in a mini-bus told us her name was Angel. Shy and nerdy as usual, I stood awkwardly on the sidelines, enchanted by Carina's magic with the kids. I was relieved, when we retreated from the merciless heat and dirty streets into the Grand Tembaga, but I was glad I had tagged along with Carina and had met some of the local people. After paddling around in the pool to cool off, I felt even better.

March 10, 2012. This morning after breakfast Franky told us he had found another helicopter. However, the only available pilot had never flown as high as 14,000 feet elevation and was not comfortable doing so. We would not fly today. Resigned to another day in Timika, Carina and I made another foray outside the hotel to buy more bottled water. Carina's relaxed attitude helped distract me from my frustration about our repeated delays.

Dennis and Carina had found enough in common to joke and laugh together. However, when I tried to talk with Dennis, he avoided my gaze and ignored my questions. After breakfast Kevin had us practice setting up one of our Marmot Trango tents in the upstairs hallway between our hotel rooms. When I tried to work with Dennis, he brushed me off with a terse, "I've got this. I've got this." *What's up with this guy?* I wondered, feeling rebuffed for reasons I did not understand. Qobin seemed to be more interested in his laptop than preparing for our climb. Unlike most of my previous mountaineering trips, this group did not seem to be coming together as a team. I tried to convince myself, *the delays and uncertainties are frustrating for all of us, perhaps explaining our lack of cohesiveness.* Still, I felt uneasy.

Kevin and Franky arranged for us to visit a country club. The drive through the countryside was a nice break from the noise and dirt of Timika. Lunch was not ready when we arrived, so I suggested a walk around the spacious grounds. Kevin nodded OK, but he and the others stayed inside.

I wandered outside in the humid heat on paths along expansive mowed lawns and thick patches of jungle. The jungle was intimidating yet intriguing. I felt a deep respect for the earlier explorers who had hacked their way through what looked like impenetrable walls of strange plants and giant trees. I had mixed feeling about flying to Base Camp – guilt about not earning the summit by hiking through the jungle mixed with relief about avoiding the jungle's rumored dangers.

I walked past huge bromeliads with stalks bent into graceful arcs of red and yellow flowers. Towering trees flaunted fin-like buttresses and draperies of vines and epiphytes. Exotic bird calls filtered through the thick canopy overhead. I looked up and tried to spot the songsters, but they remained hidden. A strange sound rose and fell repeatedly, like an electric motor winding up and then winding down. *Some kind of cicada?* I wondered. The air had a moldy yet alive scent. Intrigued, I tried to imagine what new curiosities we would find nearer the peak.

Looking across one of the spacious, well-groomed lawns, I could see people in the distance playing golf, probably highly paid executives from the Freeport Mine. The contrast between the luxurious golf course and the gritty poverty of Timika was jarring. Sweating from the heat, I went back inside the cavernous dining room. Near the entrance was a small library of worn books. While waiting for lunch, I leafed through them. Most were old novels in English and Dutch, echoes of colonialism or reminders of home for today's foreign visitors.

At last lunch was ready. We filled our plates from an even wider offering of delicacies than we had enjoyed in Denpasar. We were the only guests at a feast that could have fed dozens of people. Had Kevin and Franky arranged this especially for us? I tried to appreciate this colonial-style luxury, but part of me disapproved of such extravagance in a poor country like Papua. Also, I felt as though I were being appeased with luxuries I did not want. I had come here to climb, not to eat rich food. Each day Franky had told us, "helicopter tomorrow, I guarantee," but when the next day had come, he had a new reason why we could not fly. The days were slipping by, and we were no closer to Carstensz Pyramid. On past mountaineering trips waiting and uncertainty had been part of the experience. Today, reminding myself of this did not make it easier.

The others were also frustrated by the delays. Dennis said he hated being at the Grand Tembaga. He wanted to fly back to Denpasar and stay at the Sheraton Hotel there. Carina also wanted return to Denpasar to be with her new husband. Qobin was spending more time on his laptop. The group was on the verge of flying apart – literally and figuratively.

That evening at the Grand Tembaga we met again with Franky. He talked animatedly about Indonesia's five different districts and people who live high in trees. He avoided our questions about when we would leave Timika. Apparently nothing had changed; we still had no helicopter access to Base Camp.

Winging It

Gradually the conversation shifted to the logistics of hiking through the jungle. Franky said that we could fly by small plane to a dirt runway near the village of Sugapa (pronounced SooGAHpah). From there we would hike for five days to Base Camp, spend a day climbing the mountain, then hike back to Sugapa in four days. Each day in the jungle would take 10 to 12 hours of strenuous hiking over rugged, thickly forested terrain. Summit day would require an even longer day of 12 to 25 hours, possibly in heavy rain in temperatures near freezing. If we left Timika tomorrow and had no more delays, we would return to Timika on March 22, after our trip was scheduled to end. Kevin would have to cancel one of his other guiding commitments, something he was reluctant to do, but he was willing, if our group wanted to hike to Base Camp.

After Franky left, Kevin described the jungle's challenges in more detail. We would need to hire about ten Papuan porters. Because tribal warfare could flare up at any time, the porters would bring their wives and children. We would have to pay the porters and buy enough food to feed them and their families as well as ourselves. Local tribes could demand payment from us to cross their lands. The porters could strike for more money or abandon us in the middle of the jungle. Being kidnapped by hostile tribesmen was a possibility. We would be in a remote region. If any of us were kidnapped, injured or sick, we would need to self-rescue. Kevin had not done the jungle hike before. Perhaps he was simply giving us his guide company's standard caveats, but he seemed very pessimistic. I felt as though I were watching a TV ad about a new drug that promised miracle cures yet warned of countless life-threatening side effects.

The hike sounded dangerous and scary. Even so, I was tired of being jerked around by the on-again, off-again guarantees of helicopter access. I was ready to give the jungle hike a go. The other team members slouched in their seats, eyes downcast. Their body language told me, they were not keen on the hike, before any of them spoke. Then Qobin reminded us that his wife was 36 weeks pregnant. Carina repeated that her mother had pancreatic cancer. Both she and Qobin did not want to be inaccessible should anything go sideways with their family members. Dennis was not keen on the hike, because he was concerned about problems with his knee. I seemed to be the only one who was interested in trying the hike.

Qobin claimed that his boss was very influential and could get us helicopter access. I was skeptical. Also, I wondered how Franky would react to Qobin taking over part of his job as local operator. However, when Franky rejoined us later in the hotel lobby, he seemed delighted. "Qobin has done a good thing! You fly to Base Camp in military helicopter!" Franky said excitedly. *Fine*, I thought, *if it could really happen, I was on board.* My hope soared again. I ran up the stairs to Carina's and my room to prepare.

After several hours of private meetings among Franky, Qobin, and someone Franky called "the commander," Kevin told us that helicopter access was no longer an option. Qobin had already left the expedition. Kevin said the rest of us could hike to Base Camp or end the expedition now. Earlier today Dennis and Carina had seemed against the jungle hike. *This trip is over,* I thought. My heart sank. To my surprise, Dennis and Carina said they would do the hike. My spirits rocketed from despair to joy. I ran upstairs to prepare for an early departure the next morning.

In the dark hallway, as I was unlocking the door to Carina's and my room, I glanced to my right. Several doors down, I could see Kevin's silhouette, as he was unlocking the door to his own room. Head down, shoulders rounded, his posture was the epitome of dejection. A warning bell went off inside my head. Kevin did not want to do the jungle hike. I tried to convince myself that he was just tired like the rest of us, tired of all the delays, tired because it was nearly 11 p.m., but the warning bell still rang.

March 11, 2012. "No planes fly today, because it's Sunday," Franky told us this morning at breakfast. *Another delay, another day in Timika,* I groaned to myself. However, Franky had brought us rubber boots for the jungle hike, a tangible sign of progress. I already had my own mud boots and decided to use them instead of the flimsy ones Franky had brought. He said he was about to go shopping for food we would need in the jungle. Dennis reminded Franky that he ate four boiled eggs every day for breakfast. Finally we were making progress toward getting near the peak.

After the daily ritual of dodging traffic to cross the street to buy bottled water, I used an ancient PC under the stairs behind the hotel's front desk to email friends and my sister. I wanted them to know that we were leaving Timika at last. The PC was very slow, but my emails were eventually sent. Afterwards, I paddled around in the little pool, sometimes swimming, sometimes running in slow motion in the waist-deep shallow end. If it was good conditioning for race horses, I reasoned, it was good conditioning for me. Carina joined me. Dennis came and sat on the pool's edge. Carina convinced him to swim with us. For the first time in days, Dennis smiled and seemed almost friendly. Perhaps our team was coming together at last.

That afternoon I saw at least a half dozen small planes flying overhead. *What happened to "no planes fly on Sunday?"* I thought bitterly. *Someone is jerking us around again. Get over it,* I coached myself. *Tomorrow we will fly to Sugapa and start hiking toward the mountain. We are making progress!*

March 12, 2012. As usual, the muezzin's electronic call to prayer woke me up at 4:15 a.m. I could not get back to sleep, but I made myself stay in bed. The next few days could be very demanding. I needed to rest, even if sleep eluded me. I envied Carina's ability to sleep through Timika's pre-dawn noise.

Our morning drive to the airport was quiet. We each were in our own heads, like the electric stillness just before the starter's gun at a foot race. At the Timika Airport, we unloaded our packs and duffels and followed Franky into the domestic terminal. It was smaller, darker, and grubbier than I had remembered when we had arrived from Bali. Then I realized that we had arrived from Bali at Timika's international terminal.

As we waited for our flight, the dimly lit waiting area filled with passengers, mostly Papuans plus a few Indonesians. Most Papuan men, women, and children wore T-shirts and shorts, the result of missionary work in the 1960s. Their bare feet were broad and tough from a lifetime of going without shoes. Though most adults were several inches shorter than me, the men had well-defined upper bodies with bulging biceps and lean, sinuous legs. The women were stout from years of childbearing and hard work. Many women carried a large string bag supported by a strap across their forehead. Children were lean and slender. Some Papuans reminded me of Australian aborigines with deep-set, dark eyes, beaky noses, and short, tightly curled black hair. Other Papuans had large eyes and softer, more rounded features. I wondered whether the sharp-featured people and the rounded-featured people belonged to different tribes.

Sweat soaked through my long-sleeved shirt and hiking pants. My feet slipped inside my rubber mud boots, as sweat saturated my socks. I drank all the water in one of my one-liter water bottles and resisted drinking from my other bottle. I wanted to save some water, until we could locate more in Sugapa.

I found an empty spot in a bank of plastic seats and sat down. A Papuan woman came over and indicated with gestures that she would like a picture taken of her with me. I smiled and nodded. She sat down next to me, squashed her body against mine, and draped her arms around my neck, while her friends chattered, laughed, and pointed at us. I felt uncomfortable, not being accustomed to such physical closeness with a complete stranger. Then I felt a bit guilty about the times I had photographed local people. *Had I been insensitive or intrusive?* I hoped not. Acrid cigarette smoke flowed into the waiting area from Papuan smokers standing in the doorway. The smoke burned my raw throat and sinuses, symptoms of a cold that had started last night, a new worry about beginning our challenging jungle hike. I preferred to be alone with my own thoughts, but I smiled wanly at the Papuan woman, not wanting to spoil her fun, as Carina photographed us.

After a long, restless wait, Kevin got the signal that our plane was ready. We grabbed our climbing packs, wove through the crowd of waiting passengers, past security guards, and exited a chain-link gate from the terminal to the airstrip. Excitement replaced the torpor of our indefinite waiting, as we speed-walked toward the little plane.

We each climbed the plane's steep, narrow boarding ladder and squashed ourselves into cramped seats, a single seat on the left and two seats on the right. In my seat on the left side of the plane behind the cockpit, I held my climbing pack on my knees. I could see the pilot adjusting switches and levers for take-off. The plane's engines roared, the runway slid past my window, and vibration inside the plane suddenly stopped, as we became airborne. We were on our way!

We flew over a broad, muddy river, curving like a python below, leaving the dull glint of metal roof tops in Timika behind. Our little plane cut through layers of clouds, as it gained elevation over thickly forested, steep mountains. I craned my neck, trying to catch a glimpse of Carstensz Pyramid, but it remained hidden in the clouds. After about 40 minutes, we seemed to be circling, flying repeatedly over a narrow green valley, which I glimpsed through breaks in the clouds. Then we were flying over flat terrain again, where the broad river below looked familiar. I could see the dull glint of metal roof tops. We were landing on a paved runway, not the expected dirt landing strip near Sugapa.

Confused, I exited the little plane in a crouch, trying not to fall down the steep ladder. My team mates and I walked back to the domestic terminal in numb silence. *What had happened? Why were we back in Timika?* Inside the terminal Kevin told us that the pilot did not have good enough visibility to land the plane on

Sugapa's dirt runway. My rational self I knew that risking a crash in poor visibility would have been crazy, but my irrational self was angry after the past several days of hopes that had been repeatedly raised and then dashed.

Inside the terminal building was very hot and stuffy. Angered by this most recent setback, I could not bear to stay inside. Outside the terminal building I found a scrawny little palm and sat listlessly in its thin strip of shade on muddy grass. *What now?* I wondered dully. My skin began to burn from the midday sun. I went back inside and joined the others. No one had much to say.

During a long wait for our duffels to be unloaded, we walked to a shabby patio near the terminal entrance and sat drinking warm Coca Cola. Kevin asked whether we wanted to try again tomorrow. Dennis repeated his concern about his knee trouble. Also, he had bought an older building in London and was renovating it as a guest house for visitors during the Olympic Games in London. He was eager to return to London and oversee that project. Carina repeated her concerns about her mother's pancreatic cancer. I asked Kevin, "Could you run the hike for just me?" "No, that's not an option," he replied in a tone that signaled finality. I could understand his response, but I was very disappointed and angry. We had not gotten close enough to the mountain to see it, let alone climb it. "OK, then it's over," I said firmly, trying to be reasonable. "Let's go back to Bali."

From Bali, I hoped to get a flight to Sydney and climb Mount Kosciuszko, the highest peak in Australia, before I headed home. If I summited Kosciuszko, I would complete the original Bass list of the Seven Summits. Then my former colleague, Tom, could release our news alert announcing that I had become the oldest woman in the world to complete the Seven Summits. I would have preferred to finish with the more challenging Carstensz Pyramid, but since that was not going to happen on this trip, I hoped to at least try for Kosciuszko, before I met the press at the Salt Lake Airport.

Our small-plane pilot came over to our table and said he could try again to fly us to Sugapa, but we would need to leave now. I snapped out of my dark reverie. *Another chance at Carstensz*

Pyramid? I'm in! Hope began to sputter back to life. After a tense pause, Kevin told the pilot that the group had decided against it. The pilot's shoulders sagged. He turned and walked away. Again, my hope crashed and burned.

"Now I feel bad about ending the expedition," Dennis said with a wide, teeth-flashing smile that seemed incongruent with the current mood. Perhaps his smile was masking nervous discomfort. Carina echoed similar concerns. Trying to keep the edginess out of my voice, I said, "You guys have major concerns about the jungle hike. I respect that. I am out voted. I don't like it, but that is how it is. Let's go back to Bali." I tried to picture myself in their shoes, but I was still angry. Perhaps it showed.

They wanted to discuss it further. *There is nothing more to discuss. Let's move on,* I thought impatiently. While the others sat listlessly sipping their drinks, my engines were racing. If I was going to figure out how to get to Australia and climb Mount Kosciuszko before meeting the press at the airport in Salt Lake in a few days, I needed to get on it – now.

Everything seemed to move in slow motion. Kevin said we could do nothing more today. He arranged for a driver to take us to a secure compound of restaurants and shops outside Timika. It was nice of Kevin to do this for us, as we all were sick of Timika. However, after we arrived, all I could do was walk in circles like a caged lion. Feeling an eruption of angry frustration building in my chest, I walked to the edge of the forest out of earshot from the others and roared into the nearby trees. It didn't help; I felt no better. I wanted to be anywhere but here. I was bad company for my companions and myself. I knew it and felt bad about it, but my dark mood would not lift.

Blessings in Disguise

Back home in Salt Lake City I tried to reframe my disappointment and frustration about the aborted Carstensz Pyramid climb. *If the other team members and the guide had been so reluctant to try the jungle hike, perhaps they had saved me from myself and my compulsion to complete a project,* I reasoned.

A few weeks later Mountain Trip refunded less than half of what I had paid them. My anger bubbled up again, pulling me back into frustrations I had just started to move past. Mountain Trip claimed they had had "expenses." I was sure the trip had cost them something, but I did not see how these "expenses" could add up to 9,500 USD. I considered suing them. However, I did not want a reputation among mountain guide companies as a trouble maker. I was angry, but I was also ready to put this experience behind me and try to find another Carstensz Pyramid expedition to join.

I learned that Adventure Consultants was planning a Carstensz Pyramid expedition in August, 2012. When I emailed them, they replied that their expedition was already full, but they could put me on a waiting list. This was too ironic. Their March trip had collapsed, after climbers had dropped out. Now I could not get on their August trip.

I wanted more certainty than being wait-listed, so I did
an Internet search for other Carstensz Pyramid expeditions.
International Mountain Guides (IMG) had a Carstensz Pyramid
expedition beginning in early July, 2012. I had climbed both
Aconcagua and Kilimanjaro with IMG in 2007. Both climbs had
been good experiences. When I emailed IMG, they said they had
room for me on their July Carstensz Pyramid expedition. I was
back in the game!

IMG offered only the jungle hike option. Like Adventure
Consultants, they had tried the helicopter option and had found
it to be too unreliable. IMG described the jungle hike as a "real
adventure." On my March trip to Papua our guide's descriptions
of the jungle hike's dangers had filled me with dread. Yet pictures
on the IMG website intrigued me. Images of exotic forests, their
trees furred with emerald green moss, climbers caked with mud
grinning for the camera with barefoot Papuans fanned the embers
of my decades-old dream of having a jungle experience. Clearly,
IMG's marketing of the jungle hike worked on me.

With only three months to prepare, I got right on it. I sold
enough mutual funds to pay for the IMG expedition. I found airline
tickets to Denpasar, Bali, where the expedition members would
meet, at a good price and bought them. I read IMG's training
notes written by Jason Edwards, who had led several Carstensz
Pyramid expeditions via the jungle hike. Jason wrote:

"Think of Carstensz Pyramid as the ultimate CrossFit or
adventure challenge course in the world….we will jump, leap,
slip on roots, drop suddenly hip deep into mud, have to balance
on 30 foot historic stick bridges, which present opportunities for
unexpected twists, strains, over-stretching, and various soft-tissue
injuries. Being flexible is one of the most important things you
can do to prepare for travelling through this kind of terrain."

My anxiety began to resurface. I was not sure my 65-year-old
body was up to the challenges Jason described. I had a bit of wear-
and-tear arthritis and tendonitis in my knees as well as facet arthritis
in my lower back. My balance and agility had diminished over the
years. Deterioration in my depth perception had compromised my
ability to estimate distances, especially while down climbing and

jumping across gaps. *Would I be able to keep up with the rest of the team through the jungle?* I wondered. *Are my rock climbing skills good enough to reach the summit?*

Jason's experience gave him a lot of credibility, so I took his training suggestions to heart. To counter my anxiety, I trained regularly at a local gym and increased the difficulty of my workouts. I added an agility drill of my own design to help prepare myself for the jungle hike. At the gym I set a bench-press bar crotch high, then practiced climbing under and over it as quickly as possible, first in my running shoes, then in my mud boots and while carrying my climbing pack loaded with increasing amounts of weight.

For the summit climb I sharpened my skills on actual rock. Starting in late spring, when my friends started climbing outside, I joined them. My climbs were embarrassingly awkward and unskilled. I was shocked by how much I had forgotten about climbing rock, something I had done regularly a decade previously. *What had happened? How had my skills deteriorated so much? Duh,* I reminded myself, *when I had not practiced speaking the little French, Spanish, or Hindi I knew, it had slipped into less accessible corners of my mind. Why would rock climbing be any different?* I realized that the opportunity to climb outside on rock before another try at Carstensz Pyramid could be a blessing in disguise from the failed March trip.

My climber friends were patient and did not seem to judge me, as I crept timidly up easy climbs. When climbing once a week did not improve my skills, I hired Anna Keeling, a local, certified mountain guide. Anna and I were about the same height, but she was leaner, more muscular, stronger, and at least 20 years younger than I. Though I was fit and strong for a woman of my age, next to Anna I felt like a weakling with too much fat around my middle. Friends later told me that Anna was a nationally rated mountain bike racer and expert skier who certified other professional guides. She was too modest to mention these impressive accomplishments.

Anna was patient with my hesitant climbing. On one steep wall, I gouged my knee, as I lunged for a hand hold. The knee bled, dripping down my leg and onto the rock face. It was not serious, just messy, but that day it freaked me out. I froze, unable to get my

mind in gear and find holds I could trust. My anxiety grew from a
dull buzz to a shrill scream inside my head, *I'm scared, I can't do
this, I hate climbing, why am I doing this!?* Though I had not said
a word aloud, Anna read me like a book. She called down, "Carol,
you have to get your game face on and just do it." She was right.
I clinched my teeth and made a move, then another, and another.
It wasn't pretty, but I got up that climb.

Over the weeks, my confidence waxed and waned like some
kind of weird moon. During the waning phases, I felt unqualified
to climb Carstensz Pyramid and wondered whether I had been nuts
to sign up for it. During the waxing phases, I told myself, *I just
need to tell the negative self-talk to shut up and get on with my
training.* A new climbing friend, Ellen Leis, and Anna both said
my climbing was slow but okay. Their assessment helped prevent
my self-doubt from overwhelming me.

My short rock climbs helped refresh my skills, but I needed a
dress rehearsal for the long day of climbing on summit day. I wanted
to practice wearing the leather belay gloves and the mountain boots
I planned to use on Carstensz Pyramid, which would be too cold to
climb with bare hands and light-weight rock climbing shoes. The
West Slabs on Mount Olympus in the Wasatch Mountains near
where I live was a logical choice. Though this route was rated
only 5.5 according to the Yosemite rating system, and was easier
than the normal Carstensz Pyramid route, the West Slabs ascends
1,600 vertical feet and could take all day, like Carstensz Pyramid.
About two weeks before I left for Papua, I arranged to climb the
West Slabs with Alex LeMieux, another local, certified guide, as
Anna had already left for New Zealand, where she, her husband,
and their young son lived for six months of the year.

Alex and I started early in the morning. Our approach to the
climb involved a bit of bushwhacking and route finding. After a
couple of minor wrong turns, we scrambled up a shady couloir (a
narrow, mountainside gully) with patches of hard, steep snow, then
to the base of the climb, where we each tied into a 60-meter rope.
What I could see of the route looked less steep than it appeared
when viewed from the valley floor. Much of it had cracks and

edges for feet and hands, yet some sections looked quite smooth. As Alex and I began our climb, I was not sure whether my mountain boots would stick to the smooth rock.

Alex led the first pitch, while I belayed him. A pitch is a section of the climb, up to the length of the rope between climbers, to a safe place, where the lead climber can belay the following climber. Belaying is a technique of managing the rope to protect a climbing partner during a fall. When it was my turn to climb, I was pleasantly surprised how well my boots stuck to the rock, even when I used only the very tips of my toes. I felt like a ballerina en pointe creeping up the rock. On subsequent pitches, I looked for smaller holds and steeper lines to test my boots' limits.

After our 10th pitch, Alex and I untied from our rope, coiled and loaded it into his pack, and scrambled up to the ridge. The summit was not much further up the ridge's spine to our left, but we each had summited Mount Olympus many times before, so we decided to descend, before it got too late.

We rappelled down the slabs. Alex scrambled down first to locate the first rappel anchor, a sling around a big tree with a steel ring through which to thread our rope. Rappelling is a technique in which the climber backs down a steep rock wall, feet flat against the wall, while controlling the feed of the rope through a friction device attached to the climber's harness. Alex, then I, managed each of several successive rappels smoothly. We were scrambling down the couloir off rope, when I slipped and lost my foot holds. Hanging by my fingers from a rocky ledge, I froze, paralyzed with fear. Alex helped me get my feet back on the rock, so I could climb down safely. I felt like a fool, but Alex did not treat me like one. Even after that embarrassing moment, I was pleased to have climbed the entire day carrying a climbing pack and wearing the boots and gloves I planned to use on Carstensz Pyramid.

The IMG training guidelines suggested hot yoga to increase core strength and flexibility. In recent years heat and humidity had made me feel weak, unmotivated, and even unwell, so I had avoided trying hot (or Bikram) yoga, though several friends had enthusiastically recommended it. During my last practice climb with Anna, she told me about a special deal at a local yoga school, 10 continuous days of Bikram yoga for 20 USD. I decided to give it a go. Twelve days before I left for Bali, I signed up.

While I was still employed with the Utah Department of Health, I had practiced YogaFit yoga regularly for about seven years in our in-house fitness room. I had even taught a basic yoga class there once a week for two years. YogaFit teaches us to be patient and kind with ourselves. I had found the gentle, YogaFit approach to be a beneficial counterpoint to the traditional, no-pain, no-gain fitness training I had used for decades.

At my first Bikram yoga class I made a timid entrance. Very lean guys wearing only fitted black trunks padded barefoot in the lobby. I felt self-conscious, as I wrestled my yoga matt, towels, water bottle, and gym bag into the semi-dark studio. Heat hit me like a blast furnace. In a rear corner, I stripped down to sweat band, jog bra, and running shorts, resisting the urge to compare my aging body unfavorably to the bodies of lithe, younger yoga practitioners. Sweat ran from every pore, trickling through my hair, down my chest, back, arms, and legs. *Let it go,* I coached myself. *You have sweated before. Not this much,* my inner whiner whimpered, as sweat saturated my sweat band and poured into my eyes. Other practitioners were lying on their backs with their eyes closed on their mats. That looked like a good idea, so I did the same.

Lying there staring at the ceiling, my usual pre-yoga meditation took over. I relaxed, deepened and slowed my breathing, and quieted my mind. Curiosity replaced some of my anxiety. *What would this first Bikram yoga class be like? What would I learn?*

Suddenly someone opened the studio door. Bright lights came on and stung my eyes. A male voice rang out. "Welcome! I'm Stan. Stand up! Is anyone new to Bikram yoga?" I scrambled to my feet and timidly raised my hand along with a couple others in a sea of experienced practitioners. "Follow along, and do what you can," Stan advised us. "If you need to, stop and rest a moment." *I can do that,* I thought. I relaxed a little.

Then we began. Unlike YogaFit classes, which consisted of long, slow flows accompanied by the instructors' gentle coaching,

"If it hurts, don't do it; don't bounce, don't lock your joints," Stan barked militaristic commands, "Bend back, way back, fall back; now bend forward, more, lock your joints, more, bounce! Lock your joints!" Stan signaled the end of a pose or stretch with a sharp hand clap like a gun shot, which made me flinch.

Within minutes, sweat stung my eyes and blurred my vision. I thought my eyeballs would drown. I clawed sweat from my face at every opportunity simply to see. When I tried to stand on one foot, lift, and grab the other foot as instructed, my foot slipped out of my hand like a greased fish. The constant drip, drip, drip of my own sweat drove me nuts. *Let it go, it's only sweat,* I reminded myself repeatedly.

Several times I was tempted to stop and rest, but I took a deep breath instead and kept going. Finally, all the poses, flows, and breathing exercises were done. Lying on my sweat-soaked towel in final relaxation pose, I felt a quiet sense of triumph. I had survived my first 90-minute Bikram class. I would be back tomorrow. As the days passed, the classes became not easy, but easier. My flexibility improved more than I expected in such a short period of time.

Meanwhile, IMG emailed a link to a video of Papuans demonstrating for more autonomy from Indonesia (see www. youtube.com/watch?v=2qonI4-5iA8). The video showed large parades with some Papuans wearing tribal regalia and carrying traditional spears or bows and arrows. Others carried separatist flags and banners. Though the parade appeared to be peaceful, the video was unnerving, as Indonesia had a recent history of ruthlessly suppressing even peaceful demonstrations like this one. The political situation was out of my control, so I tried to focus on factors I could control, like my fitness training, to prepare for this trip.

Time sped up and slowed down erratically, as my departure day approached. Unexpectedly, John Pieper with Gregory, a locally owned company that makes packs, found the only size small of a canary-yellow, 50-liter Alpinisto climbing pack in North America and got it to me before my departure day. I had admired Alex's copy of this pack, when we climbed the West Slabs on Mount Olympus. Alex must have told John about me. This new pack was perfect, as our Carstensz Pyramid guides wanted us to wear bright colors in the jungle, so we would be easier to see in the dense, dark foliage. I was delighted and grateful for John's last-minute gift.

June 29, 2012. I woke up early, unable to sleep. The first of my series of flights from Salt Lake to Bali was in the evening, so I had the day for last-minute preparations, before the airport shuttle picked me up. I rechecked and repacked my gear for the last time, trying to get my jungle hiking and climbing gear down to the 44 pounds we would be allowed for the final flight from Timika to Sugapa. I failed spectacularly. My gear weighed 97 pounds. *Why do mountain guide companies do this?* I grumbled. *They insist we bring every item on their equipment list, but then my baggage always weighs too much.* On past trips, the guides had helped me decide what to bring on the climb and what to leave behind during the gear check, before we left our last hotel. That thought eased some of my annoyance and anxiety.

I would carry my mountain boots and knee-high mud boots in my new yellow climbing pack as my carry-on bag. To conserve space, I stuffed each boot with other items that would be difficult to replace if lost, such as my prescriptions and digital camera. Around the boots, I crammed my journal, a small bag of toiletries, passport, cash, travel documents, and debit card. Everything else, I divided evenly between two duffels, so if one went missing, all items of a particular kind would not be lost.

To calm my pre-departure jitters, I went to my gym for a short, easy workout. There would be few opportunities to exercise during the long flights and lay overs in airports. After a light lunch, I picked spinach from my garden and gave bags of it to my neighbors. I watered my lawns, vegetable garden, and fruit trees one last time. I tried to nap, hoping to stockpile sleep before the trip. No luck. I kept remembering things that needed to be done and jumped up to do them. I had to smile at this familiar pattern of pre-trip restlessness. I was turning down the air conditioning, when the airport shuttle pulled into my driveway. I shouldered my climbing pack and grabbed my two duffels, wrestling them through the front door into the hot, summer evening. Preparation was over. The trip had begun. A familiar sense of relief swept over me.

A Family of Climbers

June 30, 2012. After long flights and lay overs, I felt sleep-deprived and dull, when I arrived at the airport in Taipei just after dawn. I fought drowsiness in the slow lines to clear customs. I found a ladies' room, took my morning meds, brushed my teeth, and washed my hands and face. A brisk walk around the airport in the early morning, before it filled with other travelers, helped reawaken the sense of excitement and curiosity I enjoy about travel. I admired large banks of lavender moth orchids, exhibits about indigenous peoples of Taiwan, and displays of luxury goods I did not want but could admire. When shops began to open, I browsed through their aisles. Some offered finger-tip-sized free samples of dusty lavender-colored bean cakes. They were bland and not very sweet but interesting.

Hours later, the enclosed waiting area opened for my flight to Denpasar. I was ready for a break from hours of walking, so I went inside to sit down and read. I looked up occasionally, scanning the waiting area for people who looked like they might be members of my expedition – strong, lean men, carrying climbing packs, and wearing hiking pants or mountain boots. A narrow-shouldered man with glasses and very short salt-and-pepper hair grinned broadly, as he walked toward me, his right hand outstretched for a handshake. He introduced himself as Jason Edwards, the expedition leader for this climb.   He was older than I had expected, yet not as old as I, and he had a youthful energy that I liked.

Jason introduced me to Dan Zokaites, the other IMG guide. Taller and broader than Jason, Dan looked very young.   With his long, brown hair in a thick pony tail, wide-set, blue eyes and glasses, he looked more like a member of a college rock band than a guide.   Later, I learned that Dan was 27 years of age and had a degree in biomechanical engineering with a focus on robotics. Dan had the lean build, deep tan, and easy, relaxed gait of a man who used his body as well as his mind to make a living.   With Jason and Dan was Dave Mauro, one of the other members in our expedition.   Just shy of 50 years of age, Dave had a broad, bear-like build with the thick, muscular arms of a guy who worked out with weights.   His butterscotch colored hair gave Dave a boyish look that contrasted with the smile lines at the corners of his eyes. Jason, Dan, Dave, and I found seats and chatted off and on, getting to know each other.   When announcements squawked over the loud speakers in Chinese and heavily accented English, we would pause mid-sentence and listen.   None of us could decipher these announcements, but there was comfort in numbers.   If we missed our plane, at least we would miss it together.

We arrived in Denpasar mid-afternoon, deplaned, and wove through crowds to the baggage claim area.   When we spotted one of our team members' duffels, we worked together to load it onto one of our baggage trolleys, our first team-building experience. After the hassle of lost checked luggage during my trip here last March, I was relieved after all of our duffels had been found.   And, at least as importantly, we were already working together as a team.

As we pushed our baggage trolleys through the terminal, I smiled at small reminders of my previous trip – bright little offerings of flowers, rice, and coins in shop doorways, statues of deities and demons, long, polished marble walk ways, crowds of slim, graceful, local people, some in Western white shirts and trousers, others in traditional sarongs and Islamic caps, contrasting with plump European and Australian tourists in shorts. *Was that a rat that I just saw out of the corner of my eye scurrying across the airport lobby? Whatever it was, it was huge, nearly the size of a possum and about as ugly.* I made myself focus on steering my heavily loaded trolley through the crowds, as I had just narrowly missed a small boy who had darted in front of me. The heat and humidity were not as fierce as I remembered from my March trip. Even the rat did not detract from the airport's reassuring familiarity. It felt good to be here, to give Carstensz Pyramid another try.

We managed to squeeze all our duffels, carry-ons, and ourselves into a couple of dark SUVs with tinted windows. Jason and Dan had reservations at the Bali Rani, a hotel close to the airport for about 150 USD a night. Dave and I waited in the hotel lobby, while Jason and Dan checked in. A large bronze sculpture of running stallions, slim and graceful as Balinese dancers, dominated the lobby. I circled the sculpture slowly, admiring the sinuous horses.

Dave and I agreed that this hotel was too pricey for the few hours we would have until our 2 a.m. flight to Timika. We decided to share a room at a cheaper hotel suggested by our taxi driver. I was a bit nervous, as I had just met Dave. When we arrived at the hotel and checked in, Dave specifically asked the clerk for a room with two beds. *Good,* I smiled to myself, *Dave and I are on the same page.* Also, paying about 40 USD each was easier on our respective budgets than the Bali Rani's rate. I was tired from days of long flights and little sleep. I knew I should go to bed immediately. However, after our respective showers, we sat on our separate beds – as chaste and proper as shy teenagers -- and talked.

Dave was divorced and had two grown sons. One son was gay. Dave said he would not have wished that for his son, but he accepted it and tried to be supportive. His acceptance seemed genuine, and I liked him for it, especially after hearing accounts from other gay people, whose families had rejected them. Dave was in a long-term relationship with Lin who, unlike Dave's ex-wife, supported his mountaineering dreams in spite of her anxiety about his safety. I was glad for him, that he had such a good relationship.

Dave worked in personal finance, but his passions, in addition to mountaineering, were acting, stand-up comedy, and blog writing. I was fascinated. I have always admired people who could act, because I was painfully shy as a young woman, and I have no talent in the performing arts. Writing is hard work for me. I enjoy talking with other writers and learning from them.

I overcame my usual shyness, took a bold step, and asked Dave whether he would like to hear a little from my first book. Sitting on my bed, propped against pillows, I cleared my throat nervously and read my book's opening paragraphs aloud. Dave said he liked how I started the book. I felt confirmed and supported, especially by a fellow writer. Dave reciprocated by reading to me his blog about leeches. I found his writing to be full of sly wit. My own writing seemed overly serious and drab in comparison. His blog reminded me to appreciate the humor and absurdity of life.

Dave also talked about finding ways to make other people happy. He said he liked to find someone who needed a little extra support on mountaineering trips and help that person succeed. I liked Dave's generosity, but I hoped I would not be that person. I did not want to be a nuisance or liability to the other members of our expedition. Dave also shared how he had learned to accept help from family and friends, while he was recovering from a bad leg fracture and was wheelchair bound for several weeks. *I could learn from Dave's example,* I told myself. Accepting help graciously, when I needed it after a series of bone surgeries had been a challenge for me.

I enjoyed talking with Dave. He was smart, funny, perceptive, generous, compassionate, and ruggedly masculine, an attractive combination. *If only he were not already in a committed relationship.... The good guys always seem to be unavailable,* I thought wryly. *Perhaps that is why I like them. I feel safe with unavailable men.*

July 1, 2012. After we landed in Timika, our driver met us at the airport and drove us to the Grand Tembaga, the same hotel where my previous Carstensz Pyramid team had stayed in March. In the hotel lobby members of the staff recognized me and greeted me as "Miss Carol." I grinned and shook their hands. Being remembered felt nice. I glanced behind the check-in desk for the slow, temperamental PC that had been my link to the outside world during my previous visit. It was gone. I felt a sense of loss. If I wanted to email my sister and friends back home, I would need to find an Internet café. I had not seen any during my previous visit.

I dumped my duffels and climbing pack in my room upstairs and went back down to the dining room. The breakfast buffet was the same combination of Western and Indonesian dishes I remembered from last March. I filled a plate with fresh papaya, yogurt, stir fried vegetables, and spicy Indonesian chicken. It was as good as I remembered.

After breakfast, we had our first expedition meeting and introduced ourselves. Jason and our three Indonesian guides, Steven Liwe, Jemmy (pronounced Jimmy) Makasala, and Raymond Rengkung, had hiked through the jungle to Base Camp and summited Carstensz Pyramid several times recently. This was reassuring, especially after my previous guide's lack of Papuan jungle experience and his description of its dangers.

Steven was our head Indonesian guide. He wore such a serious expression he seemed to be scowling. Jemmy had a degree in mechanical engineering, but he chose to make a living as a guide. Jemmy was quiet, but he smiled often. Raymond told us that he was in training to become a "priest" in three Protestant denominations. He was the most gregarious of the three Indonesian guides. Steven and Jemmy were lean and wiry. Raymond was a little chubby around the middle, but he looked strong.

The Schmidt family made up half of our group of 12 climbers. They were a family of giants from Berkeley, California. Dori, 46 years of age, was the shortest, at six feet tall. She had the clear-eyed gaze of a capable woman who was used to holding her own in a family of tall, energetic men. She had mid-length brown hair, the well-defined arms of a rock climber, and a ready smile. Dori had trained as a biologist and had run the introductory biology lab for undergraduates at University of California, Berkeley, until her sons were born.

Dale, 47 years of age, was well over six feet tall and proudly claimed to have lost 30 pounds before this trip. He still looked a bit portly. *First impressions can be deceiving,* I reminded myself. Dale owned a business that helped students prepare for the MCAT, an exam taken by applicants to medical school. *His business must be doing very well,* I thought, *to afford this trip for his family.* Dale talked enthusiastically about some of their previous climbs, such as the Moose's Tooth in Alaska. Dale also told us about living in Indonesia and Libya as well as a dramatic emergency plane landing he had experienced as a boy.

The four Schmidt brothers were all over six feet tall, including the 15-year-old twins, Nathaniel, or Nano, and Josh. Nano, his thick, light brown hair in a brush cut, met us with a clear-eyed smile. Josh, his twin, had dark hair, was quiet and heavy-browed like his dad. Jeremy, age 17, was also quiet and looked like an older version of Josh. Ben, age 19, was dark-haired, the tallest of the brothers, and had his mom's open, friendly manner. He was in a pre-med program at UCLA, my own alma mater. Later, we enjoyed talking about UCLA and his courses. All the sons had the strong, supple bodies of young men. I reckoned they all would do well on this trip. They were full of restless energy and alternated between annoying each other with pokes and jabs and affectionately draping an arm over each other's shoulders. When their energy got too boisterous, Dori weighed in with quiet authority.

Denis (pronounced DehNEE), age 47, was an urban planner from Alma, Quebec. A little taller than I and thin and wiry, Denis had very short brown hair and wore glasses. He seemed confused, when we spoke to him. Often he would hesitate, and then say "OK" with a quick bob of his head. I could not tell whether "OK" meant he agreed with what had been said, he understood but did not necessarily agree, or he was simply acknowledging that he had heard but did not understand. *Fair enough,* I reminded myself, *I often do not distinguish between acknowledgement, agreement, and understanding, when I say "OK."* Denis' labored English was difficult to understand, and trying to converse with him was challenging. Then I remembered my visit to France in 1988, my own struggles to revive my rusty high-school French, and some of the local people's impatience with me. I made a mental note to be patient with Denis.

Pal (pronounced POWell) from Norway had just turned 50 and looked fit and lean, like he did a lot of cross-country skiing, which it turned out he did. I later learned that he was the head of a large cardiology program in northern Norway that treats 5,000 heart patients and performs 1,800 coronary stent procedures annually. He and I later enjoyed conversations about his program, a center of excellence that practices telemedicine, uses two helicopters and five fixed-wing planes to transport patients from remote locations, and performs robot-assisted surgery. As a prominent physician, I reckoned he was a guy who was used to being in charge. I liked his ready grin and sense of humor as well as his energetic intelligence.

Roger spoke with a Texan twang. He was from Dallas, where he worked as an in-house patent attorney for a major telecommunications company. He was in his early 50s, had sandy hair, a beaky nose, and was a bit chubby. Again I reminded myself that first impressions can be deceiving. Chubby guys had sometimes finished ahead of me in marathons. Roger said he wanted to try his five-toed running "shoes" in the jungle, all the rage among "barefoot" runners. I was skeptical, but Jason replied, "That might work." I liked Jason's optimism.

We were expecting another team member, Ivan (pronounced eeVAHN) from the Dominican Republic, but he was stranded in Hong Kong with visa troubles. That sounded ominous. I wondered whether he would arrive in time to fly with us to Sugapa.

After our introductions, Jason gave an overview of the trip and general information about the cultures we would encounter. Some of this information I already knew from my previous trip, but Jason also filled us in on more recent events. A special election had been called. Because elections were often associated with violence, Jason advised us to stay inside the hotel. Papuans on mind-altering drugs sometimes attacked others without apparent provocation. Roving gangs of thugs had hacked people with machetes, and the Indonesian army and police had shot others.

If we insisted on going outside the hotel, Jason advised us to go in groups. He suggested we wear neutral-colored clothing, as bright colors might have tribal or political significance. He told us to avoid anything that looked like a voting area, people who looked like soldiers or police, people who appeared to be on drugs, crowds, and side streets. Jason added that Westerners were unpopular, because Papuans often assumed they were affiliated with the Freeport Mine, which many local people saw as having taken much and given little back. This advice was similar to Kevin's last March but more detailed making the rationale behind it easier to understand. Or perhaps the advice had had more time to sink in and make better sense to me by now.

Jason gave us specific advice on how to behave around Papuans. He told us, "Be low key, passive, smile a lot, and avoid conflict." He said that on a previous trip, his group had seen one of the male porters brutally beat his wife. The porter had knocked her down and kicked her in the head and face. Jason and the other members of his group had resisted the urge to intervene. Instead, they had quietly watched. When the beating ended, they had treated the woman's injuries. A solemn silence spread through our own group. I was not sure that the others could stand by, if something similar happened on our trip. I had similar feelings, yet I was not sure I would be willing to take on one or more enraged Papuans armed with machetes or poison-tipped arrows. I felt like a coward, but there it was, the honest truth.

Our original plan had been to fly from Timika to a dirt airstrip near the village of Ilaga. From there, we would quickly hike above the thick jungle to a plateau of about 12,000 feet in elevation. The rapid gain in elevation would be challenging, but it would spare us the greater risks of additional days in the steep, mountainous jungle. However, 50 local people had been killed recently in a tribal war near Ilaga. The Indonesian Army was there now, trying to suppress reprisal killings. The area is closed to outsiders including us. The Ilaga option was now off the table.

Jason told us that we would fly to Sugapa instead to begin our hike. My heart sank. Starting in Sugapa meant we would spend more days in the jungle. After hearing Kevin's stories about broken legs and the need for self-evacuation during my previous trip, I would have preferred the Ilaga route. *Don't dwell on catastrophes, which might not happen,* I coached myself. *Think of it as an adventure.* Jason said that the jungle hike from Sugapa would be challenging, but we would become better forest walkers with practice, a note of optimism that helped calm my anxiety.

On summit day, Jason continued, we would climb steep limestone for 10 to 24 hours. There would be no place to camp or bivouac during this climb. If we were lucky, the fixed lines and Tyrolean traverse would be in good condition, and we could use them. Fixed lines are ropes attached to the wall of a climb. Climbers can move up the fixed lines with an ascender attached by a leash to their climbing harness. As they move up a wall, climbers slide their ascender up the fixed line, where it catches and will not slide down, providing a portable anchor in case of a fall. A Tyrolean traverse is one or more ropes spanning a gap. Climbers can attach their harness to the traverse and then hand-over-hand themselves across the gap. If the fixed lines or Tyrolean traverse were not useable, the climb would be more difficult and possibly take even more time. Rain or snow could also slow our progress. Long hours in wet, cold conditions could put us at risk for hypothermia, a dangerous lowering of core body temperature resulting in loss of coordination and mental focus among other things, not good when climbing steep, exposed rock. *Sobering challenges,* I thought, fighting a sense of inadequacy.

After our expedition briefing, the guides came to each of our rooms and did a gear check. I had been given a room of my own, which I appreciated. I had unpacked my gear and organized it on one of the two single beds. Jason helped me make final decisions about what to bring and what to leave behind in Timika.

Even after the gear check, my duffel that the Papuan porters would carry weighed 45 pounds, well above the maximum of 37 pounds. I would have to leave behind more stuff without omitting anything essential. I had gone through this dilemma on previous expeditions, but it was still frustrating. I raked my fingers through my hair in exasperation, which only made it stick up in silly-looking spikes and did not solve the problem.

I considered taking out some of the 12 pounds of snacks the expedition notes said to bring. On past climbs most expeditions had provided more food than I could eat. However, on a few expeditions food had run out. Too little food was more likely to be a show stopper than too much food, I reasoned. In frustration I ate some gorp, my favorite mixture of roasted almonds, raisins, and dark chocolate M & Ms. *Emotional eating, bad SilverFox!* I scolded myself. In repentance, I skipped lunch and spent more time trying to pare down my gear.

Jason had suggested that I could carry my 12 pounds of snack food in my climbing pack through the jungle. That solved the overweight duffel problem, but then my pack weighed over 30 pounds, more than Jason recommended for the strenuous jungle hike. At least the snack food, as well as my supply of Citrucel and Gentlelax, which I used to manage irritable bowel symptoms, would get used up, as the hike progressed. I hoped the first days of the hike would be easy, when my climbing pack was at its heaviest.

Déjà Vu All Over Again

July 2, 2012. I awoke at 4:15 a.m. The nasal muezzin call to prayer reminded me that I was in Timika. I was tired but couldn't sleep, so I got up. A small, black lizard darted among the folds of my bed's rumpled sheets. *How long had it been there?* I wondered, *all night?* I tried to catch it to turn it loose outside, but it was too quick for me. I wasn't crazy about having a lizard in my bed, but it seemed harmless. I was more likely to hurt it, accidentally rolling over and squashing it, than it was likely to hurt me.

At breakfast, Jason told us a plane had crashed on the dirt airstrip in Sugapa and was preventing incoming flights from landing. There would be no flights to Sugapa today. *Here we go again with the delays,* I thought glumly. *Déjà vu all over again,* as Yogi Berra had famously said.

Jason suggested that we meet in his hotel room and set up our harnesses for fixed-rope climbing. We started with our Purcell prusik, which is a locking carabiner attached to the climber's harness by a leash whose length can be easily adjusted using a prusik. A prusik is a friction knot made from loop of climber's cord wrapped around a rope two or three times. For the Purcell prusik, the friction loop is part of the leash wrapped around itself. A climber can use a Purcell prusik as a personal anchor when resting during a climb, while preparing to rappel, and as a backup attachment on a Tyrolean traverse. Before this trip I had found instructions on how to make a Purcell prusik on the Internet, had made one, and had practiced using it during my climbs with friends back home. However, I was happy to have Jason check to be sure I had tied mine properly and was using it correctly. For pictures of the Purcell prusik, please see https://www.google.com/search ?q=Purcell+prusik+picture&client=firefox-a&hs=zsV&rls=org. mozilla:en-US:official&channel=fflb&tbm=isch&tbo=u&source =univ&sa=X&ei=_SPDU7axFJeiyAT0_4HICQ&ved=0CDQQ7 Ak&biw=1093&bih=506 .

Next, we set up our yoke, a length of climber's cord about an arm span long with an ascender on one end and a carabiner on the other. The carabiner acts as a safety, keeping climbers attached to the fixed line, while they remove the ascender to pass each place where the fixed line is attached to the mountain. A center loop in the yoke goes through the waist loop and leg loop of the climbing harness so that the ascender and the safety are each attached on a separate leash.

Following our guides' instructions, we each set up our yoke and tested it to be sure each leash was the right length, just long enough to push the ascender and the safety up the fixed line an arm's length yet still within reach. Then we practiced on a mock-up of a fixed line, in which team mates held a length of rope, simulating where the line was fixed to the mountain, while others took turns clipping in and moving up the rope. This practice resembled a game of Twister in the crowded hotel room. It could have disintegrated into silly giggles, but we settled for a few chuckles and focused on rehearsing the skills we would need on summit day.

After our practice session, I needed bottled water. With Jason's specific advice on what to avoid, if we chose to leave the hotel, I felt a little braver than during my last time here. Dave and Roger were keen to come with me, so we would be following Jason's advice to go outside as a group instead of alone. We dashed across the busy street, dodging traffic, and went to Tops, the store I had patronized last March.

Inside I showed the guys where the bottled water was. Then we searched the aisles for snacks. I wanted something with fiber to help manage my irritable gut. I found some tiny prunes that I later discovered to be more pit than fruit. Dave found chocolate bars. They looked good, but the heat would melt them during the jungle hike turning them into an unappetizing mess, so I resisted the temptation to buy them. Also, I was not safe alone with chocolate. I would just eat it in my room instead of saving it for the hike. When I paid for my water and prunes, the young Islamic woman in her black head covering at the cash register looked familiar. "Hello, it's nice to see you again," I said. She replied with a timid smile and ducked her head. I was not sure whether she was afraid of me or simply shy around foreigners.

The guys wanted to explore more of the town. I was less enthusiastic. Our guides had advised against it. In March Carina and I had walked up and down the main street and ventured onto a few side streets. I remembered our walks as hot and miserable along streets full of smelly trash. However, the guys' adventuresome spirit was contagious.

We set off down the main street. Hordes of motorbikes, Land Rovers, and mini-buses roared past us. Passers-by on foot and on motorbikes mostly ignored us, but some stared at us intently. I could not tell whether their expressions were hostile or curious.

Side streets tempted the guys. Jason had advised us to avoid side streets. I followed reluctantly, stepping gingerly over holes and broken pavement, around garbage, parked motorbikes, and muddy puddles, past vendors selling fish and vegetables. The guys took lots of pictures, which most local people welcomed. In a twisted side street, one young vendor proudly held up a single fish about 18 inches long for the camera. The guys and I clicked away. In the same spirit, another vendor picked up a couple of small fish from his own display. Local men on the crowded sidelines laughed raucously. The vendor threw his little fish down in disgust. We all laughed. Male humor about "whose is bigger" transcends culture.

Bold roosters strutted down the muddy lanes with the elegance of trained dancers. Their bronze feathers flashed regally in the sun. They cocked their heads and looked at us with bright, confident eyes. The origin of the expression "cocky" was obvious. Dave crouched down, so I could take his picture with one of these local regents.

I spotted a young woman with a green motorbike kitted out as a mobile vegetable stall. She wore a matching green helmet. As a grower of vegetables myself, I had to have a picture. Suddenly the woman disappeared behind her motorbike. Clearly she did not want her picture taken. "OK, no picture of you," I said, knowing she probably did not understand me. I got a picture of her mobile vegetable stall without her being in the frame. A couple of passing women stood near the motorbike and smiled shyly for the camera.

In one of the crowded side streets, a small boy walked toward me holding a plastic bag filled with a muddy-looking drink, which he sipped through a straw. As he passed, he tossed the bag at me. I dodged. It splattered at my feet, narrowly missing me. Maybe the boy thought I was with the Freeport Mine. Or maybe he was just being a brat. I was annoyed. I wanted to grab him and shake some manners into him. Instead I ignored him, remembering Jason's advice to be low key and avoid conflict.

Heading back toward the hotel, a couple of young Indonesian men riding a motorbike stopped us to practice their English. Dave did most of the talking. I envied his gift for gab. Mostly I just stood there and grinned stupidly. More bikers stopped. "You with Mine?" one of the bikers asked. "No, no, we are here to hike, to see your beautiful jungle," I replied, remembering Kevin's advice last March not to tell anyone we were here to climb Carstensz Pyramid. "You with Mine," the other said confidently. "No, we are here to hike," I repeated. A crowd began to gather around us. It all seemed friendly, but I remembered Jason's advice to avoid crowds. Dave and Roger must have remembered too, as we all started to leave. "Nice talking with you guys. We have to go now," I told the crowd. The bikers politely said goodbye, the crowd dispersed, and the guys and I returned to the hotel. I felt relieved as well as a little daring.

Later that evening, we had to weigh our duffels, climbing packs, and ourselves for our flight to Sugapa. I had borrowed a small, hand-held, digital scale from Dan and had worked hard to get my duffel down to exactly 37 pounds and my climbing pack down to 28 pounds including two empty, one-liter water bottles. I packed everything else into another duffel to be stored at the hotel, while we were in the jungle. After dinner, we piled our jungle duffels, climbing packs, and ourselves into two SUVs and drove to what looked like a wholesale store. Inside we wove our way past stacks of 50-pound sacks of rice to a cargo scale with an old-fashioned dial and needle. Most of the others weighed in the 80 to 110 kilogram range. Denis weighed less, about four kilograms more than I. Dave leaned over and privately expressed his concern about Denis being "diminutive." To me, Denis looked wiry and strong, like the Sherpa porters who carry 70-pound loads up to Everest Base Camp. I reminded myself that not all wiry people are strong, just as all muscular guys do not necessarily do well in the mountains. Still, if Dave thought Denis was "diminutive," I wondered wryly, *what does that made me as the lightest and shortest member of our team?*

After our weigh in, Jason and Dan stayed inside the store to finish the paperwork for our flight, which would hopefully go as planned tomorrow morning. Our duffels would be transported to the airport tonight. The rest of us waited in the SUVs. Curious Papuans emerged from the night to stare at us through the SUV windows. They were short but strong, muscular, and very dark. Their deep-set, dark eyes glittered with curiosity.

Roger liked the necklaces several Papuans were wearing, which were a long string of tubular, yellowish beads featuring a single boar's tusk as a pendant. Roger bargained with a Papuan woman mostly in gestures and single words. The other Papuans and the rest of us watched with rapt interest. Roger and the woman settled on 30 USD. Roger put on his new necklace and thrust out his chest, pleased with his purchase. I wondered whether the woman's husband would allow her to keep the money. Suddenly a dozen of other locals wanted to sell us their necklaces. I decided to wait and see whether I could find something really cool and authentic to buy during our jungle hike.

After we returned to the Grand Tembaga, Dave realized that he had left his wallet and passport in his duffel, now locked in the store room with the scale. Dave would need to show his passport, when we left Timika, hopefully on tomorrow's flight. Steven went back to find the man in charge of the store room and retrieve Dave's stuff. Later Dave told us that Jason had tiptoed into his room and dropped his wallet and passport onto his chest. Startled, Dave thrashed himself awake, but he was very relieved to have his valuables back. He quickly forgave Jason's little prank.

The plan for tomorrow was for us to fly as two separate groups to Sugapa, a village about an hour's flight north of Timika, where we would start our six-day hike south to Base Camp. Our flights were chartered, and we might have all fitted aboard a single plane, but Jason explained that we needed to avoid the appearance of arrogant Westerners bumping local people from flights. I was silently concerned about the logistics of keeping our large group together, both during this first stage of getting to Sugapa but also during the hike and climb. *Jason has done this trip before and knows what he is doing,* I reassured myself.

July 3, 2012. Jason and the Schmidt family were supposed to fly to Sugapa today, but we had news that the disabled plane was still blocking the runway. Later we learned that the plane had not crashed, but it had damaged a tire and could not be moved. Flights to Sugapa were suspended indefinitely, until a new tire could to be located, transported over land somehow to the Sugapa airstrip, a neat trick with very few roads through the mountainous jungle, and then fitted onto the disabled plane, so it could be moved out of the way.

To ease our disappointment, Jason arranged for us to visit a large park outside Timika. We piled into four SUVs with Indonesian drivers, including Remmy, a driver I remembered from my previous trip here. He and I exchanged shy smiles, as we recognized each other from my stay here last March. At the park, light rain provided a good opportunity to try out our umbrellas. I had brought a compact GoLite umbrella from home. Jason provided larger local umbrellas to others in our group.

At the park, I left the main wide paths and walked further into the forest on muddy trails. I ran into Dori and Jeremy. As we three walked together, I thought I was pretty observant, but they noticed bugs, flowers, and fruits I had walked past. Dragonflies with maroon wings edged with black lace darted among the forest's lower-story plants. Dori picked up and pulled apart a large, orange fruit, so we could examine its insides. We admired huge trees draped in vines, moss, and epiphytes, their massive trunks bolstered by flaring buttresses. Brilliant yellow and red tiered flowers arched like the trajectories of rockets from clumps of large-leaved plants. Exotic bird calls echoed in the jungle, lush and vibrantly green in today's light rain. I felt a kinship with Dori and Jeremy due to our shared curiosity about nature.

Jeremy said he had read about leeches that fall out of trees onto people here in Papua. I had not seen any leeches here during my previous trip, so I was skeptical. Then Jeremy pointed to a skinny, black leech on the front of my shirt. It was hurling itself end over end toward my face at an alarming speed. I was not usually squeamish about creepy crawlies, but this thing flinging itself toward my eye balls was unnerving. I swatted it away with stereotypical, sissy-girl revulsion and thanked Jeremy for spotting it. The thought of it attaching itself to my face was very creepy.

We all shared a Chinese dinner with very slow service at one of the restaurants near the park. I got up to find a restroom in the building complex. Along the trail I found a large, iridescent, green beetle, bigger than my thumb, dead but undamaged. I brought it back to show to the others. Jason cautioned me, "You're a toucher. Be careful what you touch. Lots of things are toxic here." I was a little annoyed by what seemed like over-protectiveness, but Jason had a good point. I would be more careful in the future.

As the saying goes, every dark cloud has a silver lining. Back at the hotel, we learned that our flight delay had a silver lining. The mysterious Ivan, the last member of our group, had finally arrived. At the Hong Kong International Airport officials claimed that he needed a visa to fly to Indonesia, yet they would not issue one to him. By the time Ivan learned which offices to contact, it was Sunday, and these offices were closed. Resolving his visa troubles had required several international telephone calls, including one to the United Nations office. I wondered how Ivan had managed this. He must have very influential friends.

Ivan was tall and had the bulky upper body of a guy who worked out regularly at a gym. He had large, dark eyes, an aquiline nose, and very short, cropped hair. I was not surprised to learn that Ivan was a captain in the Dominican Republic Army. He looked like a military man, except he was friendlier than the stereotype of the steely eyed soldier. Ivan also ran a tourism business and guided hikes in Central America. He proudly told us he was the first person from the Dominican Republic to summit Everest. He was voluble, good natured, and quick to express his opinion. *Very Latin American*, I smiled to myself.

July 4, 2012. We had received news that the plane blocking the Sugapa runway had been moved. The Schmidt family was scheduled to fly early this morning, so they had gotten up before dawn, while rest of us had slept in. We were enjoying breakfast, when the Schmidt brothers clumped back through the hotel lobby in their mud boots and greeted us in noisy high spirits. Their flight had been cancelled. *Here we go again,* I thought, with resignation. I did not share the Schmidt brothers' good-natured acceptance of the cancelled flight. It felt too much like last March and repeated cycles of anticipation followed by disappointment and frustration.

Jason advised us to stay at the hotel in case we had another call to go to the airport and try for another flight later in the day. Some of us paddled around in the little swim pool in the hotel's central courtyard. I climbed up and down the stairs to keep my legs in shape and did yoga in the hallway to stay flexible.

I missed the PC that used to be under the hotel lobby stairs. I wanted to email my friends and my sister. The hotel manager explained that the PC had broken. He kindly let me use the PC in his office. Its Internet connection was very slow, but I was able to send email. I hoped he understood how much I appreciated his generosity.

Dave and I went across the street to Tops to buy more bottled water. My toiletry kit and daily medications for anxiety/depression disorder had gone missing, the first time that had happened in my many travels. I had a toothbrush and two tiny tubes of toothpaste from overnight kits the airlines had provided, but I still needed dental floss and a small hair brush. I was not going to even try to find replacement medication, since I did not trust the quality or purity of any drugs I might find here. I had been trying to wean myself off that medication for the past six months. *Maybe it is the time to go cold turkey,* I told myself.

I was trying to focus on the positive, but I was still worried. This trip with its many risks and uncertainties was not an ideal situation to stop taking a medication I had used for 16 years. I reminded myself, *worrying about becoming anxious is not helpful.* Then I chuckled at my own silly joke and tried to put anxiety out of my mind, which about as easy as the old joke about trying to stop thinking about a pink elephant. After looking in several shops, I finally found and bought a cheaply made hairbrush for the equivalent of about 4 USD. I pulled off its six-inch handle to save weight and space. I could not find any dental floss.

The Other Side of Nowhere

July 5, 2012. The plan was for Jason and the Schmidt family to try again for a flight to Sugapa early in the morning. Dan and the rest of us hoped to fly later in the day. Again, while we were at breakfast, the Schmidt family returned to the hotel, their flight cancelled. The brothers were quieter this morning. A heavy sense of disappointment hung around them. Memories of my frustrating March trip threatened to overwhelm me with dark, angry thoughts.

Following Jason's advice, we stayed in the hotel in case we got another opportunity to fly later in the day. I did some last minute rearranging of my gear in my climbing pack and risked washing my briefs and socks in the sink, hoping they would be dry, before we left. Later in the day, the Schmidt family and Jason left again for the airport.

A few hours later the rest of us left. When we arrived at the airport, we started to get out of the SUV. Dan told us to stay inside the vehicle. He explained that we needed to keep a low profile. The waiting and the uncertainty of whether we would fly today tried our patience. We were restless and on edge. Some of the guys started to get out again and stretch their legs, but Dan again told them to stay inside the SUV. Dan went inside the terminal to find out what was going on. We waited. Finally, Dan came back and told us to get out of the SUV with our climbing packs. We were like race horses bursting out of the starting gate. We hurried through the parking area to the terminal. I dog trotted to keep up with the guys' long strides.

Inside the domestic terminal was even hotter and more crowded than when I had been here in March. Dan advised us to be careful not to bump people, as we slid through the crowd, mostly Papuans and a few Indonesians. We found a place to huddle together near the mesh gate that opened onto the airstrip. A tiny whiff of fresh air slipped through the mesh and cooled the sweat that already streamed down my face. Papuan men, women, and children swirled around us. Many men and women were wearing boar's tusk necklaces like the one Roger had bought. Most Papuan adults wore shorts and T-shirts. Nearly everyone was barefoot. A few of the older men wore cheap, rubber, knee-high boots. A few of the women wore pleated skirts that reminded me of the uniforms Catholic school girls wore 60 years ago in my childhood neighborhood. Some Papuans stared openly at us. When I smiled, a few Papuans smiled back. Most ignored us.

Photographic opportunities abounded. However, Dan had told us taking pictures could increase tensions. I did not sense any hostility, but Dan apparently did. He scolded Roger for restlessly turning this way and that, bumping nearby local people with his climbing pack. "You're doing it, you're doing it again, Roger," Dan muttered tersely. I carefully took my climbing pack off my back and wore it on my chest, so I would be less likely to bump anyone. I tried to stand perfectly still. Rivulets of sweat coursed through my hair, down my face, neck, chest, back, and legs, soaking my shirt back and my pant legs.

We did not see the Schmidt family or Jason in the crowd. We hoped out loud that their plane had taken off, and they had already landed in Sugapa. I asked whether there was time to go to the toilet. "If you hurry," was Dan's clipped answer. I eased through the crowd. The toilet was busy, so I decided returned to our group, hoping for another opportunity soon. Suddenly, Dan tensely motioned us through the mesh gate.

It was a relief to get outside into the fresh air. *We have left the terminal, so our plane must be ready for us,* I thought happily. We turned right and walked briskly in the shade of a long awning that ran the length of the terminal with the runways on our left. Then we waited.

We had not gone outside to board our plane. Dan later told us that Roger's behavior had led to our abrupt exit from the terminal. Apparently, while I tried to find an unoccupied toilet, Roger had reached for a security officer's pistol in its holster. Roger was probably just being a good old boy from Texas checking out a fellow gun enthusiast's piece. However, reaching for a stranger's gun was a bad idea even in the United States, let alone in Papua, where we did not speak the local languages, recent violence had occurred, and tensions were running high. Roger's actions had nearly gotten us all into a lot of trouble, potentially ending our trip, before it had really started. Then I remembered last March, when I had chirpily told Cowboy Boots, a complete stranger at this airport, that we were here to climb Carstensz Pyramid. Perhaps my innocent attempt to make friendly conversation had jeopardized our helicopter access and ultimately ended that trip. *I should not be too quick to judge Roger,* I told myself.

It was cooler outside the crowded terminal but not much cooler. Some of the guys stood in the sun to get a closer look at planes on the runway. When I joined them, my skin felt like it was on fire, perhaps due to increased photosensitivity from my malaria prophylactic medication, doxycycline. I retreated to the shade under the awning. Several helicopters came and went. Just the sight of them merrily flying around seemed to mock me and made me mad. They brought back vivid memories of my frustration last March. I took deep breaths and tried to exhale my bitterness.

Steven went back inside the terminal and brought us slim, little cans of Straberi soda. I drank my soda and the rest of my bottled water. With the heat and my constant sweating, I hoped we would have access to more safe drinking water soon. *At least my climbing pack is back down to 28 lbs. without the water,* I thought.

With each landing plane, a spark of hope flared inside my chest. Maybe this was our plane. Passengers descended the metal ladder to the tarmac, men unloaded cargo and then loaded different cargo into the plane, other passengers boarded, and the plane took off, leaving us earthbound. My hope sputtered and died a dozen times, a speeded up version of the March trip. *When would it be our turn?* I wondered, my mood growing more sullen with each departing plane.

I went in search of a toilet. Men in uniforms with side arms gave me directions to a toilet on the way back to the mesh gate, so I did not have to re-enter the stifling terminal. The squat toilet stank of old urine. I tried not to breathe, while I took care of business. I sloshed the grimy tiles around the slot from a bucket of brownish water, hurrying to escape the stink as quickly as possible. At least the discomfort from a full bladder was now gone.

Rain clouds darkened around us. As the hours crept by, our chances of flying today sank along with my spirits. More planes landed and unloaded. *A good sign,* I thought, trying to cheer up myself. *At least flights have not stopped for the day. But would our turn ever come?* I was glad I had kept a book to read, though it was more weight to carry through the jungle. I had time to read then use the stinky toilet again. I was resigned to another night in Timika, when suddenly Dan motioned us toward a small plane.

A pick-up truck loaded with our duffels already flanked the plane. Men were heaving our gear and other goods into the tail section. People who lived in and near Sugapa depended on supplies to arrive by air. I later learned that the many planes that had taken off before ours were backlogged flights for Papuan passengers and supplies.

I shook off the torpor from our long, uncertain wait and speed-walked toward the plane. The guys and I exchanged glances, bright with anticipation. I climbed the boarding ladder behind a Papuan boy who looked no older than ten years of age. I sat in a single seat behind him on the left side of the plane near the cockpit. The boy seemed to be traveling alone. I glanced at a Papuan man across the aisle. He stared ahead stoically. *Was he scared or bored?* I wondered. My team mates and I flashed grins at each other, as the plane taxied down the runway. The bumpy ride turned smooth, as we lifted into flight.

The plane headed northeast. Below us the broad, rust-colored river curved like a snake toward the sea, a familiar landmark from my previous flight in March. I wondered whether its odd color was due to pollution from the Freeport Mine. The plain below us soon rippled into thickly forested hills. Unlike my flight in March, this time there were fewer clouds, and we could see more of the landscape below. We could see clusters of buildings, then, as we flew over mountains, single huts and small plots of cleared land, then increasingly narrow terraces on steep mountain sides. *Creating these terraces must have taken a lot of back-breaking work,* I thought. I could barely imagine hiking through this rugged terrain, let alone making a living here, as Papuans do. *Would we have to hack our way through the jungle with machetes?* I wondered.

I craned my neck and tried to spot Carstensz Pyramid through the clouds. The peak was north of Timika, and Sugapa was north of the peak, so we had to fly past it. I had hoped to catch a glimpse of it, but all I could see was thick banks of clouds. *Not good,* I thought, as our pilot had turned back in March due to poor visibility.

Sooner than I expected, a bare ridge of reddish dirt appeared in the distance through a break in the clouds. Our pilot flew just past the ridge then turned toward it in a wide arc. *Could that be the landing strip?* Excitement rippled through our little plane. Cameras clicked. The boy in the seat in front of me seemed agitated. I wondered whether he was nervous or excited to be arriving in Sugapa. On an impulse, I passed him a piece of wrapped hard candy. He thanked me with shining, dark eyes and a cautious smile, the kind I might have given a complete stranger who had just offered me candy.

The plane angled downward sharply. The dirt airstrip rushed up toward us. I clutched my arm rests and braced myself. The plane thumped hard, bounced, thumped again, and skidded roughly. Trees at the end of the airstrip rushed toward us, as the plane bounced several more times and finally slowed to a more controlled speed. It was the scariest landing I had ever experienced. I breathed again. Dave leaned over and said, "This is further than you got last time, isn't it, Carol?"

Dave was right. I relaxed my clenched jaw and grinned at him. I released my white-knuckle grip on my arm rests. Steven added wryly, "Welcome to the other side of nowhere." *Nowhere?* I wondered, as I looked out the window at the sea of dark heads gathering around our plane and the strange vegetation. This seemed to be very much somewhere, though unlike any other somewhere I had ever visited.

Over the Rainbow

We climbed down the plane's ladder into a throng of curious Papuans crowding the dirt airstrip. Men, women, and children stared at us openly, as though we were wildlife. As a child I had been taught that staring was rude and was scolded for doing it, so I settled for sneaky little glances at the Papuans. When my glance met someone's eyes, I smiled blandly, remembering Jason's advice to be low key and friendly. Some Papuans smiled back. Others continued to stare, often with open-mouthed wonder, which made me uncomfortable. I tried to see things from the locals' perspective. The arrival of foreigners with their odd-looking clothes and mysterious duffels must be a source of curiosity and entertainment for them. Ivan and Dave were already taking pictures. I hesitated, after Jason's warning that taking pictures could create tension, but it seemed to be going OK. I envied Ivan's and Dave's easy ability to engage some of the local people.

Most Papuan men, women, and older children wore T-shirts and shorts. A few of the men wore only penis gourds, head dresses of leaves, and necklaces. Nearly everyone was bare footed. A few men carried rifles with wooden stocks or handmade bamboo bows and arrows. Toddlers wore only T-shirts and no pants, a practical arrangement in this part of the world, until little kids were toilet trained. Some men and women watched us with a fierce, steely-eyed gaze. Later I realized that part of the steeliness was due to their deep-set, very dark eyes, not necessarily a challenging, don't-mess-with-me hostility. As during my March trip, I noticed that some of the adults had rounder features and more relaxed, friendlier expressions. Perhaps they were members of a different tribe than the steely-eyed people.

While the Papuans and members of our group were checking out each other, the plane was being unloaded. At Jason's signal, we each identified our own duffel and shouldered our climbing packs. Local guys, short but strongly built, grabbed our duffels and headed purposefully up a steep, gravelly road to the top of the ridge. Jason called to us over the crowd to follow these men to the guest house in town. We set off after them, trying to keep up. None of us knew where the guest house was or what it looked like. Our porters' strides were hard to match, even with their heavier loads and bare feet. The gravelly climb from the airstrip to the top of the ridge made sweat pour down my face, chest, and legs. My sweaty feet slipped inside my knee-high rubber boots, causing me to stumble. I felt clumsy and uncoordinated.

Once we crested the ridge, we could see the village of Sugapa. On the more level, less rocky parts of the path, I could take my eyes off the trail and look around. I was surprised to see what looked like several good-sized, newish buildings of wood and stucco with metal roofs. I was also surprised to see telephone poles and lines. Jason later explained that the Indonesian government had been trying to win the hearts and minds of Papuans by improving local infrastructure, justifying Indonesian governance. Several young Indonesian men in flashy helmets and black leather jackets cruised up and down the unpaved road on shiny motorbikes. They wove around Papuan pedestrians, a few half-grown, speckled pigs, and small dogs with dingy yellow fur.

Following our porters, we left the main road on the ridge and headed downhill, passing wooden huts, some with metal roofs. Ahead of me, two young Papuan women supported an older woman wearing a sarong who limped slowly between them. Her left foot was so badly deformed that she had to walk on the top of her ankle with the toes curled grotesquely backwards. I was touched by old woman's stoicism and her young companions' assistance. Clearly the old woman was valued and cared for.

Several old women with lined faces looked over shoulder-high walls surrounding their huts and watched us. When they brought their hands to their face, I noticed that some of the women had amputated fingers. A few had no fingers, only hands like paddles with short stumps. I had learned before this trip that some of the local tribes amputated fingers as an expression of grief, when another tribe member died. The sight was still shocking. I wondered how these fingerless women managed basic tasks, such as feeding and dressing themselves. I felt as though I had somehow wandered into a documentary about life here a century ago.

We arrived at a small plywood hut surrounded with a chest-high wall of piled stones. Our Indonesian guides turned toward this hut. There was no sign, but this had to be the guest house. To enter the packed earth yard that surrounded the hut, we each climbed up a short ladder of three steps to the top of the stone wall, then climbed down a similar ladder on the other side. Apparently this arrangement was intended to keep out the half-grown pigs and dusty yellow dogs. It nearly kept me out, too. I clambered awkwardly over the fence, as my feet slid inside my mud boots, my hiking poles caught in the ladders, and my pack pulled me off balance. Just outside the guest house, the Schmidt family greeted us like long-lost cousins. The gang was all here.

A narrow, wooden front porch with a railing made of branches provided a thin strip of shade from the intense, afternoon sun. There we took off our boots, padded inside the guest house in sock feet, shed our climbing packs, and drank bottled water offered by our Indonesian guides. My mouth was dry even after swigging a half liter, so I drank more.

Most of my team mates went back outside to photograph the curious locals who were crowding outside the stone wall to watch us. I was torn. I did not want to miss anything, but I also wanted to conserve energy for the hard days ahead. Inside the guest house, I sat on the linoleum floor with my back against a wall, my legs stretched out in front of me, and wrote in my journal. When curiosity got the better of me, I made short forays onto the front porch to see what was happening outside.   During one of my forays Dori stood amid the crowd, towering over a sea of local people, smiling benignly. The Papuans seemed as fascinated with her, as she was with them.

Suddenly the noise from the crowd increased. I got up again to watch a loud, arm-waving discussion between several dozen Papuans and Jemmy. One fierce-looking man with many long Rasta braids stuffed into a big knit cap spoke loudly to Jemmy, making expansive gestures. Eventually, Jemmy handed a different man with cropped hair some Indonesian money and a plastic poncho folded in a neat square. Another local man seated next to Jemmy recorded figures in columns in a worn notebook. Then the process repeated itself, this time with a Papuan woman. She smiled happily, as Jemmy handed her money and a plastic poncho. "AahhEEE!" some of the Papuans cried, in what I later learned was their all-purpose exclamation for delight and a variety of other emotions.

Jemmy hiring porters in Sugapa, photo by Pal Tande, July 5, 2012.

Jemmy was hiring porters from the Moni (pronounced MOHnee) tribe to carry our gear, Jason explained. If Jemmy hired a man, the man's family came along, too. No man wanted to leave his family behind, as tribal warfare could break out, while he was away. He did not want to leave his family unprotected. After a couple of hours, Jemmy seemed to have hired enough porters.

Originally, our plan had been to stay in the Sugapa guest house tonight. However, our Indonesian guides were nervous about possible violence due to the special election. They advised us to leave now. We pulled on our mud boots, shouldered our packs, and climbed over the stone wall. We walked down the dirt road amid Papuans on foot, pigs, dogs, and chickens, as young Indonesian men sped past on motorbikes. We began to see fewer buildings made with modern materials and more huts made with walls of woven branches or bamboo and roofs of rough, wooden slats. A rainbow arched over a single hut on a thickly forested hill. *Over the rainbow,* I smiled to myself, feeling cheerful and optimistic about having made it this far. We had transitioned from the sedentary, waiting phase of this trip and were truly under way.

Our group strung itself along the road with Steven and Jason in the lead. I paused occasionally to photograph then hurried to catch up and keep Steven and Jason in sight. Dave, Ivan, and Denis were fine with the pace. The Schmidt's were slower, but they seemed to be savoring the sights rather than concerned about keeping up. I passed Roger on one of the uphill sections of road. He was puffing hard and sweating heavily. Today was supposed to be the easiest day of walking. Roger's five-toe shoes did not seem to be helping him today.

Jemmy stopped some of the young Indonesians on their motorbikes and hired them to give us a ride to the trailhead. One by one, members of our group climbed on behind the drivers like old pros.

I hesitated. The only other time I had ridden on the back of a motorbike was as a shy, naive freshman at UCLA nearly five decades ago. That ride had led to weird, unpleasant experiences. A big, chubby guy offered me a ride on the back of his motorbike uphill to the tennis courts, where we both were taking a tennis class. I felt bold and daring that day, as I swung my right leg over the banana seat behind him. He roared up the hill, leaning hard into the turns. My stomach jumped to my throat. Shouting over the engine's roar, he told me he was a graduate student in psychology and was studying the reactions of women, when he tied them up. "I would like you to be a part of my study," he added as casually as if he were asking me out for coffee.

As naïve as I was, warning bells went off inside my head. I firmly declined. A few days later, I returned to my dorm room after classes to find my roommate in tears. This guy had called and told her in lurid detail what he planned to do to me in his "experiments." He was waiting for me downstairs in the lobby, she said between sobs.

Normally too shy to even speak to guys then, I was outraged that he had upset my roommate who was even more naïve and vulnerable than I. I stamped angrily down seven flights of stairs and found him. He was dressed in black leathers with lots of chains. He struck an exaggerated, macho stance and gave me an I-own-you look. Usually tongue-tied around men, my anger found words. I read him the riot act. His arrogant expression melted into the quivering face of a scolded child. After my short diatribe, he turned and left without a word. I never saw him again. I had not ridden on a motorbike since.

Today, nearly 50 years later, I still preferred to walk. After most of the others had already left on motorbikes, Jason said it was several miles to the trailhead. Dark clouds threatened heavy rain. I told myself, *it is time to get past a bad experience from so long ago.*

Jason stopped a motorbike driver and waved me over. The slim, young driver shyly avoided my gaze. I tightened my pack's hip belt and shoulder straps, jammed my ball cap firmly on my head, and swung my right leg over the bike's seat. *Just like getting on a very short horse,* I reassured myself. *I know how to ride a horse.* Happy memories of my younger self galloping bareback across meadows on my favorite mare flashed through my mind. As Jason instructed, I settled my mud boots onto the passenger foot rests, grabbed the back rim of the bike seat with my right hand, and gingerly encircled the driver's waist with my left arm.

We bounced downhill on the dirt road, swerving around other motorbikes as well as Papuan pedestrians, pigs, dogs, chickens, large rocks, and potholes. We rounded a bend, sliding a little in the gravel, then headed down a steeper slope, and splashed through a rocky stream. As we roared uphill, the rear of the bike fishtailed. My heart leapt to my throat. Images of the bike crashing and falling on us, crushing an ankle or knee, fueled my fear like gasoline thrown into a fire. *Stop it! Nothing like that is going to happen,* I told myself sternly. I tried to focus on the beauty of the hills covered in thick jungle, the local people's handsome features, and rainbows that appeared and disappeared as though by magic. My emotions jumped monkey-like from terror each time the bike skidded to relief that we had not crashed – yet.

My driver was skillful, but I was not a very skilled passenger. Our downhill ride caused me to slide too far forward on the seat. I was sliding into my driver. I gripped the back of the seat, trying to keep from squashing the poor guy. Soon my left arm shook from the effort and threatened to cramp.

The wind caught the bill of my ball cap and snatched it off my head. I needed that hat. Without it, I could get badly sunburned here so close to the Equator. There were no shops to buy another hat. I shouted above the roar of the bike's engine for the driver to stop. I swung off the bike and trotted back about 150 feet, my climbing pack bouncing awkwardly on my back, my feet slipping clumsily inside my rubber boots. I picked up my hat, slapped it against my thigh to shake off the dust, and stuffed it down the front of my shirt, so it would not blow away again. The driver gave me a wan smile, as I jogged back. This time, I got further back on the seat, so I could push my boots against the foot rests more effectively and avoid sliding forward.

We roared down more hills and splashed through more streams. We came to a steep uphill section of rocky road. The motorbike ahead of us was struggling, sliding, and fishtailing, as the driver tried to climb the hill. I asked my driver to stop again. "I will walk to help you and the bike," I told him. He looked puzzled. Perhaps it was a point of honor to get his passenger up the hill, but I did not want to risk a crash. He drove part way up and waited for me. When I caught up, I waved him to drive uphill further. He looked doubtful but complied. We repeated this pattern several times, until we met at the top of the slope, where I got back on the bike.

I was gaining confidence in both my driver and myself, when I noticed a small crowd of people in the road ahead. As we got closer, I recognized members of our group standing near drivers and their motorbikes plus quite a few Papuans. Jason gathered members of our team to one side of the road apart from the crowd, where we waited for the rest of our group to arrive. Everyone else seemed matter of fact about their rides and had enjoyed them. I felt like a wuss for being scared, but it was over now. More importantly, I had taken a big step toward healing from a disturbing experience that had happened long ago. I thanked my driver, perhaps too effusively due to nervous relief.

We were at the trailhead where we would begin to walk through the jungle for the next several days. Jemmy was engaged in an animated conversation with some Papuans. Later we learned that they were members of the Dawa (pronounced DAHwah) tribe demanding a toll to pass through their land. Jemmy told them we would pay their toll, but they would have to work for it. They would supply porters to carry our gear through the forest, before Jemmy would pay anything.

Finally, the last members of our group arrived. Dale looked a bit more disheveled than the rest of us. He said he had fallen off the back of his driver's bike near the base of a steep climb. His left arm was sore, but he was OK and wanted to continue. Jason examined and palpated his arm and shoulder. They were streaked with mud and a bit scraped, but the injuries did not appear to be serious. I wondered whether Dale's fall had occurred on the same hill, where I had gotten off the bike and walked. I was relieved that Dale was OK. His fall could have been a lot worse.

Dash Into the Night

Jason gave us the go ahead to start hiking, as Jemmy finished negotiations with the Dawas. Steven led us, followed by Jason, up a trail that left the road and cut an uphill traverse above it. Though the trail was narrow and faint in places, at least we did not have to hack our way through thick vegetation, as I had imagined.

Jason had told us in our group meetings that we must keep up with Steven's pace, because Steven knew just how fast we had to go to get to our next camp, before the daily rains began. Already we were too late. I had felt the first drops of rain half an hour ago. Intermittent showers, driven by gusts of wind, now peppered us.

Steven set a fast pace. I struggled to keep up. On steep sections, slick mud seemed to repel my boots by some mysterious force. Several times I fell hard without warning. Rain came down steadily now. The trail became slicker and more challenging. I tripped over roots and rocks hidden in thick, low vegetation that covered the trail. The cloud ceiling lowered, as the evening light faded. I stopped to put on my rain jacket and then got even wetter from my own sweat trapped by the jacket's so-called breathable fabric.

I tramped along as fast as I could, trying not to fall. I fell anyway. Each time I struggled to untangle myself from thorny vines, roots, and branches to stand up, I lost time and slipped further behind Steven and Jason. I tried slowing down a little to avoid falling so often, reasoning that my overall time would be faster.

Jason had warned us that some of the local bridges were pretty marginal. The first one I crossed was made of hand-sawed planks held together with strips of bamboo. *That wasn't too bad,* I reassured myself, after I crossed it without mishap.

The chest-high pig fences that crossed the trail were more challenging. Their sharpened, upright branches threatened to disembowel me, if I slipped while climbing over them. My 32-pound pack threw me off balance, as I clambered over the fences like a hunch back, trying not to drop my hiking poles. "Why don't you step on that branch?" asked Ivan at one pig fence, as he hovered impatiently just behind me. "Because it is slanted, and my foot will slip," I replied tersely. I hated these pig fences. Climbing over them sent sharp pain through my lower back and knees. I was slowing down everyone behind me, which was embarrassing. I envied my younger, more agile team mates' ability to climb over these fences more quickly. I tried to imitate them with no success.

The simple act of walking through the jungle seemed to require an exhausting level of mental as well as physical effort. Once, when I thought I was focused on where I was placing my feet, my left foot punched through what looked like solid trail. I found myself tumbling down a steep hillside, scrabbling with my hands and feet, trying to stop my fall. I heard rushing water below me. My heart turned to ice. The thought of falling into swift water terrified me. Dori, on the trail behind me, said, "I've got her," and started to climb down toward me. She sounded so calm and competent in contrast to my discombobulated state. Humiliated, I called up to her, "I'm OK, I've got this." I had stopped my fall in an awkward, head-down position and was tangled in branches and vines. I clawed back up through the underbrush like some primeval, mud-covered creature from the Black Lagoon. Thin, wiry vines covered in thorns ripped my hands. Staring at the streams of bright blood streaking my muddy palms, I thought grimly, *this is a recipe for infection.* Meanwhile, Steven and Jason disappeared around a bend in the trail ahead, as it contoured around a steep hillside.

Steven and Jason stopped periodically and waited for the slower members of our group to catch up. Jason urged us to go faster. Even with light from my headlamp, I could barely make out the trail in the thick jungle darkness, never mind see the endless roots, rocks, vines, and branches that repeatedly tripped me and snagged my hiking poles, yanking me off balance. I stumbled on as best as I could.

Suddenly, we stopped on a little rise in the trail. Steven went ahead, traversing a steep slope of loose gravel and mud a dozen yards above a rushing river. I hesitated. Jason asked impatiently, "Why are you not going?" *Do or die,* I commanded myself. I set off, trying to remember how Steven had placed his feet. The angle-of-repose mud slid under my mud boots. I scrambled awkwardly, as though trying to run sideways up a down escalator. I was slipping down the hillside, losing ground. I felt the swift river below pulling me toward it as a magnet draws iron. I was scared.

Out of the deep dusk, a little Papuan man, who had already traversed the treacherous slope, trotted back toward me. Apparently he had seen my distress and had come back to help. With a wide smile, white teeth flashing in the dim light, he crouched in front of me and dug footholds in the gravelly mud with his bare hands. I tentatively tried one of his footholds, but my foot slipped through it like a knife cutting through warm butter. When it was clear that his steps would not hold me, the Papuan extended his hand toward me. It looked like a muddy claw in the dim light. *Trust me,* his crinkle-eyed smile seemed to say, *I'll get you across.* He was covered in mud. I was covered in mud. *We are bonded by mud,* I thought crazily, *like mud brothers.* I grasped his wrist, he grasped mine, and together we crab walked, slipping and sliding together, until we came to more solid ground. Before I could thank him, he disappeared into the darkness ahead.

I was deeply moved. The Papuan man did not have to turn around and help me. He could have stood on safe ground and laughed at my incompetence. Or he could have ignored my plight and continued on his way. We were total strangers without a single word of language in common, different in race, age, gender, culture, life experiences. He had no obligation to me. Instead, he came back across the unstable slope to help me with a level of chivalry I have rarely experienced, a reminder that we each are capable of mean-spiritedness and kindness. We can choose which to express, moment by moment.

I continued on in the dark. My rain-soaked, nylon-blend hiking pants tugged heavily at my legs. Salty sweat and mud ran into my eyes, as I tried to catch up with Steven, Jason, Dave, and Ivan, but their headlamps had disappeared around a bend in the trail far ahead.

I was alone. Before my concern could mushroom into fear, I heard quiet footsteps behind me. Instead of members of my team, a Papuan man, woman and half-grown boy caught up with me. They were probably a local family headed to their home. We exchanged side-long smiles, as they passed me. I followed them for a while, passing several cross paths. I hoped I was on the right trail, the same one as the rest of my team members. What if I accidentally followed the Papuan family on a wrong trail to their hut? Would they let me spend the night with them? How would I find my team the next morning? If I stopped now to wait for team members behind me, and they were on a different trail, I risked being alone and lost in the jungle at night. The three Papuans were the only people I could see, so I continued on with them. They walked easily on strong, bare feet, following the beam of their single flashlight, while I struggled to keep up. Like the faster members of my team, the family gradually pulled ahead of me. Eventually their flashlight beam shrank to a mere speck and then disappeared around a distant bend in the trail.

I was hiking alone on a dark, rainy night in Papua, where Westerners were resented, and violence was commonplace. I was probably lost. Discouragement and fear rose in my chest like toxin. *Should I turn around and try to find some of the others?* I continued on, crossing other trails and passing huts that were dark and silent in the rain. I crossed a packed mud clearing. The trail seemed to end at a wall of piled stones. I stopped, wondering what to do for several minutes, when Jemmy came up behind me with part of the Schmidt family. I was very relieved. I vowed to stay close to Jemmy, until we got to camp.

It seemed like hours later, when we came to another packed earth court yard. Steven emerged from the rainy darkness. He said we would stay here tonight, in what I later learned was the small village of Sunama (pronounced sooNAHmah). He pointed to a hut I had not noticed on the edge of the court yard. Relief spread through my tired body, which now ached from several hard falls and the effort of hiking over rugged, unfamiliar terrain. I pulled off my boots, heavy with mud, and left them under the hut's narrow eaves out of the rain. My boots had kept out the rain, but they had made my feet sweat profusely. I took off my socks and wrung about a cup of sweat from each. My shirt and pants were soaked through and filthy.

Jason, Dan, Pal, and Ivan were inside the hut. Though the night was not especially cold, I shivered. I looked for my duffel, but the porter who was carrying it had not arrived. I dug into my new, yellow climbing pack, now very muddy from my many falls. I found a dry base-layer top. I changed into it and hung my drenched rain jacket and hiking shirt from the hut's rafters to dry. I was still shivering from wearing my soaked hiking pants. I had packed my base-layer bottoms and rain pants in my duffel to reduce the weight of my climbing pack. Now that my duffel was missing, I regretted not carrying at least the base-layer bottoms with me. Dan gallantly insisted I wear his hooded synthetic filled jacket. It was so huge, it was like a tent on me, but eventually it trapped enough of my body heat to lessen my shivering.

Over the next hour and a half the rest of the team and most of the porters arrived, all drenched from the rain. The Indonesian guides set up MSR stoves in a back room of the hut and started dinner. From duffels that had already arrived, we took out folding, three-legged camp stools. I sat on someone else's duffel, until one of the guys graciously loaned me his stool. Sips from metal cups of hot tea began to chase the chill from my body, followed by metal plates of steaming, thread-like, translucent noodles with unfamiliar leafy vegetables, chunks of what I hoped was chicken, and wavy strips of what looked like black-edged, bracket fungus. Dinner looked a bit weird, but I was hungry, so it tasted good to me. Apparently the Schmidt brothers did not agree. They picked at their food, as Jason urged us to eat as much as we could. He reminded us that we would need to eat unfamiliar foods to keep up our strength for the jungle hike and the climb. The brothers stared dully at their plates.

While I waited for my duffel to arrive, I noticed that the guest house was made from a mixture of modern and traditional materials. Its frame of branches was tied together with strips of bamboo. Vertical rough planks formed the walls, lashed together at half height with thin strips of wood. Similar planks covered the roof like giant shingles and served as the floor.

Dale and Roger were the last members of our group to stumble into the hut. Both looked spent. Dale complained that his injured arm and side hurt more than earlier in the day. He sprawled in the middle of the hut's floor and groaned. I felt bad for him, but Jason had instructed us to clear the floor of our packs and stools and lay out our sleeping bags. The hut was barely large enough for us to sleep in two rows, packed like sardines. Working around Dale's sprawled frame in the crowded little hut made this task nearly impossible.

My duffel as well as Dave's still had not arrived, so I settled for a trip to the outhouse. At the hut's doorway, I could not find my own mud boots. Someone had moved them. I grabbed the nearest mud-encrusted pair. I flinched at having to touch them. I smiled wryly to myself; my hands were nearly as muddy as the borrowed boots, though I had tried to clean them with hand sanitizer before eating dinner. In boots much too large for me, I picked my way down a slippery slope of trampled vegetation and mud to the outhouse, a flimsy little structure of branches and torn tarps. Rough planks straddled a hole in the floor, a Papuan version of a squat toilet.

Back inside the hut, Nano offered me a place to sleep next to him. His concern and generosity touched me, though I preferred to sleep in the corner furthest from the door I had claimed for myself. Jason and Dan offered to share their sleeping pads and sleeping bags with Dave and me. I was wondering how four people were going to share two narrow pads and two mummy bags, when the porter with my duffel showed up at 10:30 p.m.. Dave's duffel was still AWOL. *Poor guy,* I thought. Dave later told me that Jason had loaned him his bag and Dan his pad. This was only the first of many instances, when our guides made our welfare and comfort their priority.

Outside the hut and under the narrow eves, I found my duffel on top of a pile of porter loads and dug inside for dry base- layer bottoms, toiletries, sleeping pads, and sleeping bag. I tiptoed back inside the hut around crowded bodies to my corner, trying not to shine my headlamp into anyone's face. My team mates were already settled in their sleeping bags and trying to sleep. Across the room, I could hear the twins crabbing at each other about who was taking up too much room. Settled into my own bag, I finally got warm. Today I had been reminded that being soaking wet for hours was a sure way to become hypothermic, even in a jungle near the Equator.

In spite of using ear plugs, some of my companions snored loudly and kept me awake. Heavy rain pounded the hut's roof, muffling the snores a little. As crowded and noisy as the hut was, it beat pitching tents after dark in the rain and mud.

Bridge Over Troubled Waters

July 6, 2012. After long hours of sleepless tossing and turning, night's total darkness faded into predawn gray. I eased out of my sleeping bag and crept on fingers and toes over sleeping forms to go to the outhouse. Outside, the rain had stopped. Streamers of fog hung among steep ridges of thick forest above and below where I stood. Smoke rose through the thatched roof of another hut several hundred yards down slope. The air smelled fresh and heavy with moisture. It felt refreshingly cool. My spirits rose. My dream of over 40 years to experience a jungle had finally come true. I was so lucky to be here in this part of the world. Though I had climbed peaks on all seven continents, this was unlike anything I had experienced.

Skirting the slickest mud, I took a few pictures. I met Dave on my way back to the guest hut. I bowed to him and gestured toward the outhouse with exaggerated courtesy. He returned my silly joke with a huge grin. Dave seemed to be as psyched as I was to be here.

Back inside the hut, others were stirring. After yesterday's mad dash into the rainy night, a few of my team mates had decided to jettison some of the items in their climbing pack to lighten their load. "Gifts for the Dani tribe," Dave explained. I too would have liked a lighter climbing pack, but I could think of nothing to leave behind.

I was a slow packer, so I got started before breakfast. I mashed my sleeping bag into its compression sack, deflated and rolled up my Therm-a-rest sleeping pad, and folded my Z-rest closed-cell pad. I went outside and searched for my duffel, which had become buried under several others under the hut's eaves. Though I had hung up my wet, muddy hiking clothes, they had not dried noticeably during the night. My skin shrank from the cold, dirty fabric, as I pulled on my pants and shirt. I made a mental note to ask the guides how to dry wet clothes in this rainy climate.

Breakfast was under-cooked mung beans in a sweet, reddish-brown sauce. The Schmidt boys sullenly picked at their beans, while Jason again urged us to eat up. Though I wished the beans were not quite so chewy and did not taste like raw dried peas, I dutifully ate two servings.

Dale told us that he was stiffer and in more pain this morning than yesterday. He had decided to leave the trip. Roger announced that he had decided to leave as well. He said, "I just don't have it in me. I guess I'm more of a cold mountain guy." Jason told the rest of us, "If you have any doubts, now is the time to turn back. Yesterday was easy compared to what is ahead. Don't wait until we get deeper into the forest, before you decide you want to turn back."

Jason's words were sobering. Last night's dash in the rain had been challenging for me. I had fallen hard at least six times in about three hours. Back home, I had often hiked over rugged terrain all day without falling once. I had not been able to keep up with Steven's pace, something Jason had told us we needed to do. Self-doubt started to creep in. However, I had been far from the last to arrive at the guest hut. I still wanted to go on. I just hoped I would become a more skilled forest walker, as Jason had said we would during our first team meeting. I resolved to keep up with Steven today and not fall as often.

We said goodbye to Dale and Roger. Raymond would walk with them back to the Sugapa airstrip and help them get a flight back to Timika. I was sorry to see them go, but I respected their decision. As a parting gift, Roger gave away his personal supply of salami, beef jerky, and cheese, "man food" the guys eagerly accepted. I was already carrying too much weight in my climbing pack and had packed my duffel to the maximum of 37 pounds, so I passed.

After we had finished breakfast and packed, we waited outside the guest hut, while Jemmy argued with the porters and some of the local people. Jason explained that some of the Dani tribe, who lived in this and nearby villages, wanted to be hired as porters, so Jemmy was negotiating with them. A growing crowd of villagers stood just beyond the hut's wall of stacked stones and stared at us. A middle-aged Papuan man wandered through the crowd, naked except for several necklaces of beads and shells, a boar's tusk pendant, a matching headband, and a penis gourd made from a section of bamboo about 18 inches long and held upright by a thin waist band. Three little yellow dogs and half-grown pigs wandered among the crowd. A woman sat and occasionally petted one of the dogs. Small boys swatted at the other two dogs to scare them away. Hanging around and watching us seemed to be the main event of the morning.

Dani people in Sunama, photo by Dave Mauro, July 6, 2012.

The Equatorial sun was burning off the cool morning mist, promising another very hot day. I wanted to start, so we could hike during the cooler hours and get the day's work done, before the daily rain began. An animated argument between Steven and our porters escalated into loud shouting and vigorous gestures. We stood with our climbing packs on, wondering what to do. One woman shouted at some of the Schmidt brothers standing amongst the porters, angrily waving them away. Jason gathered us in a group away from the Papuans. He told us to wait, until Steven gave us the signal to start hiking. He reminded us to let Jemmy handle any issues with the porters. Jemmy could speak their languages, was familiar with their customs, and knew how to manage their complaints and disputes. What the argument was about was unclear, but most days would start this way.

Leaving Sunama, left to right: Jason Edwards, Ben, Nano, and Josh Schmidt, Carol Masheter, Dori Schmidt, Dave Mauro, photo by Pal Tande, July 6, 2012.

At last agreement was reached. At 9:30 a.m., Steven took the lead, followed by Jason. The rest of us fell in behind them and hurried to keep up. Dave, then Pal, passed me. My heart sank, as they pulled ahead of me. I had resolved to keep up today, and already I was falling behind. Fighting a sense of defeat, I flailed through knee-high vegetation concealing logs, roots, and rocks that tripped me. Branches and vines caught my hiking poles and tugged at my legs. I clambered awkwardly over pig fences across the trail. With every step sharp pain jabbed my lower back and just below my knee caps. I slipped and fell repeatedly without warning. I swore loudly the fourth time I fell. The four-letter words came out unbidden and uncensored, the way a dog yelps, when it is hurt. When the guys asked whether I was OK, I tried to joke, saying "Only my pride was hurt." I apologized for my blue language. The guys chuckled and waved away my apologies.

I tried to be a good sport each time I struggled to my feet, but inside I felt humiliated and discouraged. Today's hike was supposed to be the easy part. Jason had said the hiking would get harder in the coming days. *How much harder could it be?* my inner whiner whimpered.

Ivan had told us he had guided tourists on jungle hikes. During one of our brief rest breaks, Dave asked Ivan for advice. Ivan suggested using only one hiking pole. I later tried this but quickly found that I needed two poles for balance and to ease the strain on my knees and lower back. Ivan also suggested that we "surrender to the jungle." That worked for me. Someone once defined "surrender" to mean "stop fighting." Here surrender made sense. Fighting the jungle took too much energy. Whining to myself about being covered with mud, soaked with sweat, bleeding from thorny vines, and bruised from repeated falls also took too much energy. I focused on doing whatever needed to be done at the moment with less negative self-talk, whether it was climbing over a pig fence or getting up from another fall.

Our porters caught up with us. We stepped off the trail to let them pass. About fifty Moni, Dawa, and Dani men, women, and children filed by. The three tribes did not speak each other's language and sometimes went to war against each other. We were counting on Jemmy's negotiating skills to keep the peace and avoid porter strikes.

The adults and the older children each carried a load. A typical load was one of our duffels at 37 pounds, carried in a large string bag with a strap across the porter's forehead. In addition, a porter might carry the plastic poncho Jemmy had given him upon hiring, and a weapon, such as a machete, a rifle with a polished wooden stock, or a bow and arrows. Men with the most elaborate hair styles and necklaces, perhaps indicating their high tribal status, carried smaller loads.

Woman porter with toddler, photo by Dan Zokaites, July 6, 2012

A woman porter often carried her family's scant supplies including yams, which she would roast each night over a smoky fire in camp for her family to eat. Some of the women also carried our duffels. Two women carried bare-bottomed toddlers on their shoulders in addition to their loads. The babies rode contentedly taking in the passing scenery with wide eyes. The only time I heard the babies cry was at night. Perhaps they were bored without the ever-changing scenery during the day's walk.

As we hiked, I realized that the Papuans were better equipped than I was for hiking through the jungle. My hiking pants, soaked with sweat and caked with mud, tugged at my thighs with every step. My knee-high rubber boots seemed to make me trip, slip, and fall more often than on previous climbs, when I wore my more familiar mountain boots. In contrast to my clumsy efforts, the Papuans moved easily in their cheap shorts. Their bare feet gripped the muddy ground and slippery branches in the trail like powerful claws. Their low-tech approach made sense, but I was not nearly tough enough to strip off my hiking pants and boots to travel through the jungle Papuan style.

Where the terrain was less challenging, I could relax my mental focus and lift my gaze from my feet. The foliage was an exotic mixture of the strange and the familiar. I recognized some of the variegated red, white, and green foliage as popular indoor plants back home. Other plants were completely alien to me. Sometimes Dori and I walked together and admired especially striking trees and shrubs. I enjoyed Dori's enthusiasm and obvious delight at being here in spite of the oppressive heat and difficult hiking. Her positive attitude helped to distract me from the physical discomfort of the hot, humid climate, the treacherous terrain, and my anxiety about possible dangers.

After about two and a half hours, we came to a bridge of parallel logs that crossed a river to a small island, followed by a second bridge across the rest of the river. Each span of the bridge was about 50 feet long and about 20 feet above the surging water. Neither bridge had hand rails. Our guides instructed us to cross the bridge one at a time. Steven crossed, followed by Jason. I was next, followed by

Dori and then Dave. I noticed the bridge's logs, damp from river spray, were slightly flattened on top. Not too bad, I thought, as I crossed carefully, resisting the mesmerizing sight of the muscular, brown river, coiling like a giant serpent below me. I knew that if I looked at that churning water, my fear of heights would escalate and increase the chances of my falling off the bridge.

When I reached the island, I heard a loud CREEEEK behind me, then a louder CRACK!, a dreadful silence, then a loud SPLASH!! "We have one in the river!" Dave shouted. His voice rang with urgency. Dori, who had been behind me, was gone.

My brain went blank. The roar of the river filled my ears. Then all hell broke loose. Dave, Ivan, Jason, Dan, and some of the porters rushed across the bridge to the brushy little island where I was. They threw down their packs and hiking poles and trampled through the tangled mess. Even as Jason and Dan shouted at us to stay away from the river's steep bank, Ivan and Dave hurled themselves onto their bellies on the bank's edge, first in one place, then in another, trying to spot Dori through the overhanging branches. The Schmidt brothers frantically shouted Dori's name. There was no reply above the rush of the river.

Though it was blazing hot, I went cold. *Was Dori dead or alive? Had she been swept down the river? What could we do?* I wanted to help, but I just stood there, frozen, unable to act. I felt ineffective and useless. Wanting to do something to help, I grabbed the hastily dropped packs and poles and moved them out of the way, so no one would trip over them and fall into the river. What I was doing seemed trivial. I felt guilty about not doing more to help. Nausea and numb disbelief flowed over me, as relentlessly as the rushing river.

After what seemed like a long time, some of our guys formed a human chain with one of the Papuan men at the front. After a few tries, they lowered the Papuan far enough, so he could find Dori and grab her wrists. The human chain then hauled the Papuan man and Dori up the steep bank. Dori was soaked from head to foot, but she was grinning broadly and seemed intact, arms and legs working normally. Relief flooded my body. My heart beat again inside my chest, and my brain switched back on.

Dori's rescue, photo by Pal Tande, July 6, 2012.

Jason and Dan sat Dori down on the edge of the second bridge leading off our island. Then we saw the blood, lots of it, snaking down the back of Dori's neck. This was serious. My chest went hollow. I shivered in the midday heat.

With guidance from Jason, Dori's sons took off her knee-high rubber boots, poured the river water out of them, and took off her soaked socks. Jason cut away most of Dori's beautiful brown hair to get a better look at the source of her bleeding. Meanwhile, Dan palpated her spine for fractures. "Clear," Dan murmured to Jason, who nodded acknowledgement. Dan crouched in front of Dori and put a pulse oximeter on her index finger. He continually assessed her level of consciousness by engaging her in conversation. He recorded her vital signs in a little notebook.

Dori's field treatment, photo by Carol Masheter, July 6, 2012.

I wanted to help, if only in a small way. I held the first-aid bag, handed Jason rolls of gauze, and made sure the medical supplies stayed out of the mud. The porters watched our every move intently, mouths agape. Jason field-dressed Dori's scalp lacerations, wrapped her head in gauze, and covered it with Nano's blue and white IMG buff, a tube of fabric that can be used as a hat, bandanna, or neck gaiter. Dori looked like she was wearing a clever little cap instead of a bandage that covered her entire scalp. Smiling serenely, Dori looked so normal, for a moment I imagined that her fall had never happened.

But it had happened. Terrifying as Dori's fall and injuries were, Jason's and Dan's capable management of the situation was reassuring. Our porters' help with her rescue and concern about her injuries moved me, another example of their generosity and readiness to help one of us who was in trouble, even when they had been angry with us only hours earlier. Later Dori told me some of the women porters had wept, when they learned about her injuries, because they could relate to her as a mother of four sons.

Through it all, Dori remained calm and clear eyed. She smiled, talked with the guides and her sons, and seemed relaxed. Dave put an arm around her shoulders and said, his voice breaking into a hoarse whisper, "God, you scared the hell out of me." Dori smiled serenely and patted his leg. However, I noticed her hands were unusually pale and shook a little. Her pulse oximeter showed a resting heart rate of 140 beats per minute. Rapid heart rate, paleness, and shaking were signs of shock. This situation was far from over. I went to her, grasped her forearms, and said, "Dori, you are so strong. I am so sorry this has happened to you." I felt terrible that she had been injured yet relieved that the situation was not worse. My eyes filled with tears from these conflicting emotions. Dori gave me a gracious smile.

Dori calmly agreed with Jason that the trip was over for her and her sons. However, her eyes flashed, when Jason added the trip could be over for all of us. "I can accept that the trip is over for my family, but I don't want to end it for the others," Dori said firmly. "It's not your call," Jason replied with equal firmness.

My heart sank. I didn't want this trip to end now. *Déjà vu all over again,* I thought grimly, as flashbacks from the aborted March trip raced through my mind. If there were a silver lining, it was that we would only have to hike a few hours through the jungle back to Sugapa. If Dori's fall had happened deeper in the jungle, getting her out would have been much more strenuous, time consuming, and dangerous. Besides, I didn't know how much more jungle hiking I could take. *Perhaps ending the trip now would be best,* I tried to convince myself.

Ivan protested loudly about ending the trip. "This is not a camping trip," he said vehemently. He implied that the Schmidt's were not qualified and that IMG was remiss to include them on this expedition. After Ivan had repeated his points within earshot of members of the Schmidt family, Dave said quietly, "Let's give it a rest." I silently admired Dave's willingness to speak up and head off conflict in a calm way.

In Ivan's defense, he had a lot invested in this climb. Sponsors had given him generous monetary support in exchange for photographs of himself on the summit of Carstensz Pyramid holding banners with their names and logos. The sponsors planned to use these photographs in their marketing campaigns. If we turned back now, a return trip for Ivan would be difficult, perhaps impossible, to finance.

Part of me was with Ivan. This was my third try to get close enough to Carstensz Pyramid to climb it. Unstable politics and frequent violence had recently closed the mountain to climbers. That could happen again. I already had one trip cancel before it had begun. On the second trip, we had been jerked around for two weeks, spent a lot of money, and not gotten close enough to the mountain to see it, let alone climb it. On this, my third try, I was not much closer to the mountain than I had gotten in March. I was not sure my finances or my aging body would permit a fourth try. Like Ivan, I did not want this trip to end, before we had a chance to climb the mountain.

Yet, in my heart of hearts, I knew Dori's safety was our first priority. We had to get her to a hospital for more thorough assessment and treatment of her injuries. At the very least, she had deep scalp lacerations that needed to be further cleaned and stitched. Because she had been injured in the jungle, she was at risk for serious infection. At worst she could have a concussion, possibly a fractured skull, and additional, life-threatening, internal injuries. Though Dori looked stable now, her condition could deteriorate, she could collapse, and need to be carried back to Sugapa over rugged terrain. If she needed to be carried, we all would need to help. There would be no rescue helicopter, no team of trained experts to take over. If that meant the trip was over, I didn't like it, but that was how it might be. When Ivan asked me what I thought, I spoke my truth, "I want to continue and have a chance at the mountain, but getting Dori back to Sugapa is our first priority." Ivan's response was silence. I did not know whether he was disappointed that I did not share his outrage or whether he was rethinking his own priorities. After all, he had been part of the human chain that had hauled Dori to safety.

We prepared to return to the guest house in Sunama, where we had stayed last night. The Schmidt brothers helped Dori put on her wet socks and mud boots. Jason and Dan helped her to her feet and supported her, as she fought pain and dizziness. The guides asked whether she was OK to try walking. She tried a few, slow steps then indicated she was good to go. We put Dori in the middle of our group, with Jason and Dan near her and two Papuan men supporting her by her arms. All four sons hovered near her. Ben seemed especially worried. I wondered if his interest in medicine made him more aware of how serious his mother's injuries could be.

The walk back to the guest house was slow and hot. Part of me resented retracing our hard-won miles. During one of our rests, Dori calmly said her headache was worse. *Not good,* I thought glumly. However, after our break she walked a little faster and with less assistance, all good signs that her condition was stable. Behind me Jeremy occasionally sighed and groaned. I was not sure whether he was expressing worry about his mom, disappointment about leaving the trip, weariness from our hike in the heat, or a combination of these.

Returning to the guest house took us longer than our morning walk to the bridge, where Dori fell, but it seemed a little easier. My spirits brightened a little. Maybe my forest walking skills were improving, as Jason had said they would with practice. We stopped at a shallow river and splashed mud from our boots, clothes, and bodies. It felt good to be relatively cool and clean. Within 10 minutes after we resumed hiking, I was as filthy and sweaty as before the stop at the river. *Oh, well, it was nice while it lasted,* I thought.

At about 2:30 p.m., we arrived in Sunama. We waited uncertainly, while Jemmy negotiated for another night's stay. Eventually a deal was made. We settled back into the cramped space of the hut for the rest of the day and that night. At least the porters returned with all our duffels, so we all had sleeping bags, sleeping pads, dry clothes, and food. After a cheerless dinner, we again carpeted the hut's floor with our sleeping pads and bags laid edge to edge, trying not to trip over each other. At least without Dale, Roger, and Raymond, there was a bit more room.

Jason and Dan re-examined Dori's scalp lacerations, dressed them with Neosporin I offered from my personal first-aid kit, and rebandaged her head. Dori complained that her mid back hurt. Jason and Dan had her take off her shirt and hiking pants and stand, so they could examine her for additional injuries. Large, dark bruises were already coming up on her back, buttocks, and the back of her left thigh. *She could have serious internal injuries, such as damaged kidneys, broken ribs, and liver lacerations*, I thought grimly. Dori was far from out of the woods, literally and figuratively. I was worried about her.

I had not been able to reclaim my preferred place next to a wall for tonight's sleep. I was squashed between Pal and Ivan. Pal and I both positioned our heads away from the center of the guest house, as we each had done last night. Ivan decided to face toward the center, reasoning he would have more room for his shoulders next to Pal's and my legs. After we all settled down for the night, I discovered that both Pal and Ivan were thrashers. Both tossed and turned all night like breaching whales. Twice Pal hit me hard in the face with his elbow. Every time Ivan turned over, he kicked me in the face. Both men snored loudly. My ear plugs did nothing to block their rumbles and snorts. I would have moved, but there was no other space inside the hut. Someone had moved my climbing pack, so I could not find it and retrieve my headlamp, when I needed to get up and pee. I groped around in the dark and climbed over sleeping bodies, trying not to wake anyone.

At the guest house doorway, I pulled on the first pair of mud boots I could find. I picked my way to the outhouse in heavy rain, trying not to slip and fall in the mud. In the outhouse, I did my best to aim correctly in the dark for the slot. Back in the guest house, I felt better with an empty bladder, but Pal's and Ivan's snoring and thrashing prevented me from getting much sleep. Night passed very slowly. I resolved to avoid both of these guys as future sleep neighbors.

Two Bands of Brothers

July 7, 2012. The next morning began with discussions about where we stood. First, we all met as a group. Jason stated that Dori had fallen three times her own height, had landed on her head on a boulder, and was lucky to be alive. He reiterated that Dori and the three Schmidt brothers under age 18 would return to Sugapa and fly to Timika. From there, Dori would go to a hospital in Jakarta or Denpasar for further evaluation and treatment. IMG's policy required that expedition members under age 18 years must be accompanied by a parent or guardian. Ben, who was almost 20, could decide whether to return with his family or continue toward Base Camp, if any of the rest of the expedition members wanted to continue. Jason invited the three younger brothers to talk further with him and to vent their anger and disappointment. The brothers stood slumped and unresponsive. I could only imagine what they were feeling.

Dori told us that she had had a reasonable night. Her headache was a bit worse, and she was stiff and sore from her fall, but she felt able to walk back to Sugapa. Apparently Dori's condition was not substantially worse. Jason seemed to be considering the possibility that some of us might continue toward Base Camp. These were the first bits of good news we had had in nearly 24 hours.

However, if we did continue, we would have to begin the jungle hike again, retracing our steps. We already had lost a day due to delays in our flights from Timika to Sugapa. We had lost another day due to Dori's accident, and we could lose more, if we needed to accompany her back to Sugapa. If we took five long, hard days to hike to Base Camp, one day to climb the peak, and five days to hike back to the Sugapa airstrip, we would not have a single spare day for bad weather or to rest. We would be cutting it close.

Jason told us that the jungle terrain ahead was more challenging than anything we had hiked so far. He added that any further accidents would definitely end the trip for everyone. We could not split the group a third time. He repeated that if anyone had doubts, now was the time to leave the expedition.

My resolve began to waver. I was the oldest, smallest, and slowest member of those of us remaining. I was the weakest link. I didn't like that. I was used to being among the strongest on many of my previous climbs. Self-doubt chattered inside my head. *My mountain boots may not stick to the rock during the summit climb. Maybe this trip is too hard for me. Perhaps I should turn back now with Dori and her sons. I don't want to cost the rest of the guys the summit by being too slow or being the one to have another accident ending the expedition.*

Not so many years ago, the general feeling among male mountaineers was that women did not belong on mountaineering expeditions. These men claimed that women did not do their share of carrying loads or building camps. These men argued that women caused sexual distractions, disrupting the "brotherhood of the rope." I did not want perpetuate any of these notions. I wanted to keep up and do my share as a full-fledged member of the team.

While Jason and Dan talked with Dori and her sons, I found Dave and shared my concerns with him. Dave admitted that the jungle hike had been hard on him as well. I was surprised, as he had done a good job of keeping up with Steven's fast pace. Dave reassured me that my pace was fine with him, but he did not know whether my mountain boots would stick to the rock on summit day. I would have to ask the guides about that.

Dave was more concerned that the IMG guide that would continue with us was fully committed to getting us to Base Camp and up the mountain. Dave had a good point. During my previous trip to Papua in March, the other client climbers and even the guide had not seemed fully committed to doing the jungle hike. Like Dave, I did not want to struggle through the jungle, only to have a guide who was less committed than we were turn us back, before we had a chance to climb the peak.

Dave and I joined Pal, Ivan, and Denis for another impromptu meeting. The three of them were keen to continue toward Base Camp. When I repeated my concerns, they energetically encouraged me to continue with them. "Don't worry, we will help you," Ivan said, full of Latin enthusiasm. The other guys chimed in with similar reassurances. I was moved by their generosity, but I was still unsure. I did not want to be the one who needed extra help. Yet I did not want to quit now, if I had a reasonable chance at reaching the summit without being a burden on the rest of the group. I needed an objective assessment of my abilities. I told the guys I would talk with our guides, before I decided whether to continue with them.

On the other side of the packed earth yard, I met with Jason and Dan. When I expressed my concerns, Dan locked my gaze with his steady, dark-rimmed, blue eyes and said, "Carol, you're more dialed than any of these guys." I didn't know what "dialed" meant, but it sounded promising. Dan continued, "We can work with you on the pace. Your mountain boots should be OK." The breath I had not realized I was holding came out with a whoosh of relief. I ran happily back to the little group of four guys, jumped into their midst like a gleeful child, and shouted, "I'm in, guys!" We collapsed into a team hug, laughing and exchanging knuckle bashes. A few days earlier, we had met as strangers. Now we were a team, a band of brothers.

When we all gathered, Jason announced that he, as lead guide, would go back to Sugapa with the Schmidt's. I was surprised. On my previous mountaineering expeditions, when people had to leave early, an assistant guide had accompanied them. I had assumed that as the more experienced guide, who had done the jungle hike and the climb before, Jason would continue toward Base Camp with us. This was Dan's first time here. I felt a bit uneasy about following a guide who had not done the jungle hike or the climb, particularly after my experience last March with Kevin who also had not done the jungle hike. However, Jason assured us that he had chosen Dan over several other well qualified guides for this trip for a reason. Jason did not specify what that reason was, but clearly he had confidence in Dan. Also, our Indonesian guides had done the jungle hike and the climb several times before. Dan assured us that he was committed to the hike and the climb. Any reservations I had about Dan taking over the role of expedition leader began to dissolve.

The Schmidt's were preparing to leave for Sugapa with Jason. Ben had decided to go with the rest of his family. No doubt the decision was difficult for him. I respected his choice to stay with his injured mother and younger brothers, as disappointed as he may have been about turning back.

The rest of us gathered around the Schmidt's and Jason to say good bye. I tried to think of something special to say to each of them. I thanked Jason for valuable advice, information about the local people, and capable response to Dori's injuries. To Dori, I said, "You and your sons give me hope for the future." Dori replied with one of her radiant smiles and good wishes for our climb, gracious as always. I thanked Nano for his generosity and energy, Jeremy for his curiosity about nature, and wished Ben good luck with his pre-med courses. When I came to Josh, my brain cramped, and I could not think of anything to say, except to wish him luck. At least I hope I said these things. Then the Schmidt's, Jason, and some of the porters turned away and began walking toward Sugapa.

I teared up. The Schmidt's were a wonderful family, full of energy, intelligence, and affection for each other. They had had such bad luck on this expedition. I hoped that they would have a safe trip. I hoped that Dori would make a swift and complete recovery. I hoped that they would find another happier adventure to share as a family. I would miss Dori's and Jeremy's curiosity about plants and critters. I would miss talking with Ben about his studies and UCLA. I would miss the twins, so different yet so close. I hoped that those of us who had decided to continue toward the peak could approach this band of brothers' closeness.

I would especially miss Jason. I had come to trust his previous experience with and knowledge about this part of the world. Jason sometimes talked too much and repeated himself, but I appreciated his skill in assessing and treating Dori's injuries as well as his expert judgment in our difficult situation. I would also miss Jason's boyish grin and enthusiasm.

It was time for us to head toward the mountain. Raymond, already back from taking Dale and Roger to Sugapa yesterday, led us, followed by Dan. Dan told me to follow directly behind him, so I could set the pace for the rest of the group. I told him that I felt bad about being slow. Dan reassured me that my pace would be fine. He advised me not to make a big deal about it to the others.

Raymond set a brisk pace, but it was slower than Steven's. Covering the same section of trail, now for the third time, was a little easier. We made good time to Dori's bridge – 20 minutes faster than yesterday morning. I still fell more often than I would have liked, but I got less tangled in the undergrowth when I did fall, and I got up more quickly.

When we passed the red-and-white veined bushes that Dori and I had admired yesterday morning, a wave of sadness swept over me. I missed her already. When we arrived at the bridge where Dori had fallen, the local people had already added arched hand rails of freshly cut branches. I felt a rush of gratitude for their quick response. Still, as I crossed that bridge, I felt queasy, remembering how scared I was, when Dori had disappeared into the churning river.

The four guys were in high spirits. When I hesitated or slipped at a steep, slippery uphill section of the trail, often the guy behind me boosted me up. At a particularly slick wall, I tried to jam the toe of my boot into the mud, but my foot slipped to the bottom, as soon as I tried to step up. I tried another part of the wall and slipped again. When I tried a third time, Dave, who was behind me, heaved me up on over the top without warning. I landed face first in the mud. Sharp rock bit my palms and left jaw, squeezing an uncensored groan through my clinched teeth. I pushed myself awkwardly onto my feet. "Thanks, guys, but I am fine," I said, trying to be gracious. I appreciated their eagerness to help me, but it was too much of a good thing. That said I preferred too much help over being resented, excluded, or scorned by the guys, as had sometimes happened, when I was younger. Dan added, "I think she's got it, guys." Later, I thanked him privately for his confidence in me. Gradually, the guys' overly enthusiastic help eased off.

We fell into a pattern of moving for about an hour or two then stopping for a rest break of 10 or 15 minutes. When we were moving, we climbed over, under, and around fallen trees, up and down steep, muddy ridges, and crossed rivers, fording the shallower streams and using the local people's bridges for the deeper, swifter rivers. During our breaks, we ran through our list of self-care tasks. We drank water, ate a snack, put on sunscreen, put on or took off layers of clothing, and, if needed, relieved ourselves. When Dan gave a three-minute warning, it was time to put everything back into our climbing packs, shoulder them, and continue through the jungle.

As we progressed, some of the rivers we crossed were wider and more turbulent than yesterday's. Bridges made by the local people varied in complexity and stability. Some bridges were elaborate, fragile-looking structures of parallel logs bound together with strips of bamboo. Some included arched handrails made of branches. Other bridges were a single, wet, slippery log. Sometimes a rope served as hand rail for the single-log bridges, but the rope was often positioned too high, too low, or too far off to one side to be much help.

On the bridges with hand rails I could sometimes manage my fear of heights, if I crept across slowly and carefully.

Carol Masheter crossing a stick bridge, photo by Pal Tande,
July 7, 2012.

The single-log bridges above deep, rushing rivers terrified me. They reminded me too much of Dori's fall. On my first single-log crossing I could not avoid seeing the torrents rushing below me, as I started to inch timidly across. Looking at the churning water made me feel sick. My knees shook uncontrollably. Without conscious thought, my legs folded like a newborn foal trying to stand for the first time, and I sat down abruptly, straddling the log. I moved forward by boosting myself forward using my arms. This method was slow, strenuous, and humiliating but effective. I did not want to be the next one to fall and be injured, ending the trip for the entire team.

Carol Masheter making a seated crossing of a log bridge, photo by Pal Tande, July 7, 2012.

At another single log bridge, I tried to cross standing up. Again I lost my nerve, sat down, and straddled the log. One of the Papuan porters scampered back across the log effortlessly on strong, bare feet and insisted on taking my hand. His gesture was kind and gallant, but I could not see how holding his hand would keep me from falling and pulling us both into the snarling river. Yet I pulled my feet up under me, managed to stand back up on the smooth, wet log, and coached my wildly shaking legs into less violent tremors. The Papuan man's chivalry gave me confidence to shuffle across the slick log.

Like the Papuan man who had helped me scramble across the unstable muddy slope during our first hours of jungle hiking, this man had no obligation to help me. To him I must have seemed woefully incompetent and out of place. He could have ignored me or laughed at me. Instead, he helped me with a gentle smile and asked for nothing in return. His behavior exemplified the kind of person I wanted to be but have often fallen short.

Papuan man helping Carol Masheter cross a log bridge, photo by Dan Zokaites, July 7, 2012.

After I had crossed to the river's far bank, I turned and watched Dave, Denis, Ivan, and Pal stride atop the log with steady, confident steps, taking a fraction of the time I needed to cross. My timid bridge crossing embarrassed me. I wanted to do better. I studied their methods and tried to learn from their example. One thing that seemed to help was to walk duck-footed with the arch of each foot centered over the highest part of the log's curve. When I tried this on the next log bridge, it seemed to help.

The duck-footed approach also worked on slippery rocks, branches, and logs in the trail. I quickly learned to look for these as half-buried stepping stones in the knee-deep pools of mud that we encountered with increasing frequency. When I could find and balance on these stepping stones, I spent less time sinking into mud and struggling to free my feet without losing my boots. I watched Dan's steps just ahead of me. When he did not sink, I matched his steps. When he did sink, I tried stepping somewhere else.

I studied the mud, trying to learn how to read it -- where it might support me and where to avoid stepping. Just when I thought I had it figured out, the mud would throw me a curve ball. What appeared to be a root or rock was just more soft mud masquerading as a solid step, and I would sink into the disgusting stuff to my mid thighs. Traveling through this jungle presented challenges, which were very different from those of my previous climbs. I was a beginner again, starting over with learning the most basic skills.

Another trick that Dan taught me was how to place my feet on bridges made from parallel logs. Bracing my foot against the slightly higher log sometimes kept that foot from slipping off. However, occasionally this system failed spectacularly, when my foot slipped between the logs, became caught, and caused me to take an awkward, twisting fall. Now I understood how a hiker could break a leg in this jungle terrain. Other times, I tried to use small notches made by local people in slanting logs that served as ladders up or down steep, muddy slopes. At first, when I tried to position the edge of my rubber boot into a notch, my foot slipped, and I fell. But as the day progressed, my feet held more often, and I fell less frequently. I was learning from my mistakes. Jason had been right. With practice, I was getting better at forest walking. We all were.

Later in the day, Ivan complained about the slow pace. He announced that he was used to finishing hikes in three hours, and the slow pace was "killing" him. Ivan quizzed me about how I had trained for this trip. I felt defensive, as I had trained hard and carefully. When I started to describe my training program, he interrupted me, apparently not really interested in what I had to say. Dan slid his eyes toward mine, signaling, *let it go.* I went quiet. Nonetheless, my self-doubt rose like a dark cloud. My inner critic hissed poisonously, *of course the guys could move more quickly through the forest, if you were not slowing them down.* I tried to convince myself that I was protecting Ivan and the others from exhausting and injuring themselves, but I still felt bad about being the slowest. Again I resolved to move as quickly as I could without getting hurt.

In the late afternoon we arrived at a hillside covered with several large piles of freshly cut logs and branches. Our porters were making a framework from long, thin trees, which they tied together with strips of bark and bits of old rope. The porters covered the framework with a large, blue plastic tarp. They cut ferns with their machetes and carpeted the muddy ground under the tarp with fresh fronds, a charming touch. This blue tarp shelter became our kitchen and dining area. Three small mountaineering tents, which would be our sleeping quarters, were already pitched uphill from the blue dining tarp.

A second framework covered with a large, orange tarp became the porters' cooking, dining, and sleeping area. They roasted yams over a smoky fire at one end of their tarp for their dinner and tomorrow's lunch. As evening came, the day's oppressive heat eased, and the air turned cool. Some porters wrapped themselves in a piece of thin cotton fabric they used as a cape and huddled near their fire.

I could hear the sound of running water. I found a way through thick trees to a small, clear stream behind the sleeping tents. The bank down to the stream was steep and slippery, but it was only about six feet above the water, so I grabbed overhanging branches and lowered myself to a narrow beach of boulders and gravel. I dipped a tentative hand into the water. It was clear and cold but not as cold as some mountain streams I had bathed in. I took off my muddy boots and sweat-drenched socks and waded into the stream gingerly on tender feet. I splashed water onto my boots and rubbed off as much of the sticky mud as I could with my hands. I rinsed my sweat-soaked socks in the stream, wrung them out, and draped them over a nearby branch. Emboldened by the refreshing effect the cold water had on my tired feet, I shed my mud-caked pants, then my mud-splattered shirt, and rinsed them in the current. I splashed my face, arms, and legs and scrubbed off mud and sweat as best as I could without using soap, shivering and trying not to slip on the slick stones underfoot. The cold water snapped energy back into my tired body. I felt like a new woman.

I wanted to strip off my briefs and bra, but I heard someone approaching through the jungle. I settled for crouching down into a cold pool in my underwear and scrubbing my body with my hands. Dave came to the stream bank and looked questioningly for a way down to the water. I stood up, showed him where I had come down, and offered him a hand. Dave took it graciously. His acceptance reminded me that I needed to be more gracious about accepting help from others. I did not have to be a one-woman show all the time. Also, it felt good to help Dave, even in this small way, as he had tried to help me earlier today.

I could see that Dave was looking around as though he were searching for another pool. I sensed that he felt awkward about bathing, while I was there. I was pretty much done with my washing, so I pulled on my wet trousers and shirt and hauled myself back up the stream bank, just as Denis was approaching. I showed Denis the way down to the water. Then I left to give the guys a bit of privacy.

As I returned to the sleeping tents, I began to shiver in my wet clothes. I took them off, hung them on nearby brushes, and put on a dry base-layer top and bottom. The daily rain began just then. The first heavy drops were cold enough to sting. My wet clothes would never dry in the rain, so I pulled them on over my dry base layer and scrambled downhill over the piles of downed trees and branches to the dining tarp. Jason had suggested wearing wet clothes over a dry layer as a way to dry them. I had been skeptical, but my wet shirt and pants actually began to dry, while I stayed warmer and drier than I had expected to be.

We gathered under the blue dining tarp for a team meeting. IMG had provided a small canvas cot to use as a table. It, along with collapsible, three-legged camp stools, were unexpected luxuries that helped keep ourselves and our food out of the ever-present mud. I spread open a stool, placed it near the cot table, and lowered my haunches onto it cautiously. One of its legs suddenly sank into the soft mud under the fern carpet, nearly dumping me backwards. I grinned ruefully, as I scrambled to regain my balance. Dave was lowering himself onto a stool near me. Just as I started to warn him, Dave's stool threw him onto his back. He laughed long and hard, as he picked himself up. I admired his willingness to laugh at himself.

Over dinner, Dan summarized our progress through the jungle today. We had gained and lost about 3,000 vertical feet and had covered about seven miles in seven hours. *Geez, that is pathetic,* I thought. Back home in the Wasatch Mountains, my friends and I can often cover twice that distance with the same elevation gain in less than seven hours. However, Dan told us we had done well. Then I felt better. Dan also filled us in on tomorrow's schedule, when we would get up and have breakfast, when we needed to be packed and ready to leave camp.

Sharing sleeping tents is sometimes awkward on mountaineering trips. I didn't want to monopolize my new friend, Dave, or lead him to think I was chasing him, so I was quiet, when Dan raised the topic over dinner. Dan said he didn't want to share with anyone who snored. I also didn't want to share with a snorer or a restless sleeper, especially after being kicked and elbowed by my neighbors in the Sunama guest house last night. I said I didn't snore or thrash around in my sleep. Dan shot me a tentative look and gave me a little nod. I guessed that meant we were tent mates.

After dinner, Dan and I claimed the smallest of the three sleeping tents that the porters had pitched. As we moved our packs and duffels into it, Dan said we could change tent partners later in the trip, diplomatically giving us each an out, if this arrangement did not suit us.

Dan set off to dig a pit toilet. We had decided as a group to share a pit rather than dig individual cat holes. We reasoned that a shared pit of known location would lessen our chances of stepping into each other's messes. After days of constipation, a mild case of diarrhea meant I had plenty of messes to contribute. I made sure all went into the shared pit, even if it meant multiple traverses over an obstacle course of waist-high downed trees between my sleeping tent and the pit. When I returned, Dan was settled in our tent writing GPS waypoints and observations about the terrain we had covered today in a notebook. I settled into my sleeping bag, hoping to catch up on sleep.

True Generosity

July 8, 2012. When I awoke, I noticed ice inside my water bottle next to my head. Outside the tent on my way to the pit, I could see ice crystals spreading across the mud like feathery swords. Their graceful, lacy arcs filled me with a quiet sense of joy and wonder. It had been colder last night than I had realized. I had been almost too warm inside my sleeping bag. Thick jungle hid the fact that we were camped at about 9,600 feet elevation, high enough to freeze at night even this close to the Equator.

Back at our sleeping tent, Dan was awake. He said he had been cold last night in his sleeping bag and had slept in his synthetic fill parka. I offered to loan him my thicker parka, but he said he would be OK. As I struggled to stuff my thick sleeping bag into its compression sack, I wished I had brought a less bulky bag like Dan's. However, our highest camp at nearly 14,000 feet elevation could be a lot colder than here. I might appreciate my warmer sleeping bag later.

I had no appetite for breakfast. Under the dining tarp I made myself eat Muesli, a chewy mixture of coarsely milled oats, dried fruit, and nuts, soaked in reconstituted powdered milk. I usually like muesli but not today. Jemmy reminded me to smile. I gave him an exaggerated grimace, hoping he would understand my joke. Dave joined us. He teased Dan about preferring that the route to our pit toilet at our next camp not resemble a steeple chase. Dan explained that he had located the pit behind logs and piles of branches to give people a bit of privacy. *Life is full of trade-offs,* I chuckled to myself, *in this case ease of access versus privacy.* At least I was not the only one who found the log-strewn route to the pit toilet challenging. When I could not eat any more, I went back to the sleeping tent to finish packing. Jemmy settled the daily quarrel with our porters and gave us the signal to start today's walk toward the next camp. I shouldered my pack and followed Steven and Dan, while the rest of the guys fell in behind me.

Today the terrain we covered was more rugged and challenging than yesterday. Dan made suggestions to help us hike more efficiently. For the steep uphill slopes, Dan recommended that we never lift our hiking poles above shoulder height to conserve energy. I moved my hands down my poles' shafts on the steep uphill sections, keeping my hands low and using the poles like foot-long daggers, which worked well for me. Dan also recommended that we use our poles behind our feet to push rather than pull ourselves uphill. This worked less well for me. If I did not keep my poles ahead or at least even with my feet, the pole tips would tangle in the vegetation and pull me off balance, sometimes causing me to fall.

Negotiating steep downhill chutes was even more challenging for me than uphill climbs. The downhill chutes were full of branches and roots that grabbed my boots and threatened to pitch me face down into rocks below. I would instinctively grab the nearby vegetation to control my descent. Savage little thorns ripped my hands and made them bleed. I looked for branches without thorns along with rocks and roots along the walls of the chutes to brace my hands and boots, trying to channel my descent into a controlled fall.

From my assigned position behind Dan, I could hear the guys working hard behind me, slipping and sliding, gasping for breath, especially on the steep uphill climbs. When we paused briefly, I turned to see how they were doing. Their faces poured sweat. Their shirts were soaked through, as though someone had doused each of them with a bucket of water. Dave made a wry joke about the heat. I replied, "Welcome to 24/7 Bikram yoga, fellas" remembering my days of Bikram yoga torture before this trip. Though it had been a challenge for me, it seemed to have improved my tolerance for heat and humidity psychologically as well as physically.

Steven stopped at a little spring that shot clear water from a green bamboo spout, a trace of human ingenuity in this vast jungle. The guys filled their bottles and drank the water without treating it. They raved about how clear, cold, and refreshing it was. I was tempted, but with my gimpy gut, I played it safe. I added an iodine tablet to my spring water and made a mental note to add an ascorbic acid tablet at least an hour later to mask the nasty iodine taste.

By late morning we were on a high traverse on a steep hillside above a swift river. The route looked dry and solid. I was congratulating myself on falling less, when suddenly the ground under me disappeared. *What the ... ?* I was falling head first through dirt and branches toward the swift river far below. Ivan, who was behind me, dropped to the ground and grabbed for my left calf just as a tangle of branches stopped my fall. Loud shouting from several of the guys exploded inside my confused brain. My head was lower than my feet. I twisted to right myself, grabbing thorny vines. A couple of our Papuan porters rushed over, ready to help, as I scrabbled awkwardly through branches and roots up onto the trail.

I was covered with mud. A large L-shaped tear in my hiking pants exposed my right buttock. My muddy hands were bleeding. When the guys asked whether I was OK, I said I was, but the fall had unnerved me. As we moved forward along narrow ledges above the snarling river far below, my knees shook. I took tiny steps in a half couch and clung to vines, roots, and rocky hand holds on the steep hillside on our left, afraid of falling again.

The trail that had collapsed under me had seemed solid. Now I doubted my budding ability to read the trail and find solid footing. Dan instructed me repeatedly to stand up on downward sloping rocks and trust my feet, but my fear of falling shouted down his advice. I repeatedly reverted to my timid crouch. Fear made me tense and irritable. After one of Dan's scoldings, I flipped him the bird behind his back. Then I felt ashamed of my childish, crass behavior. I tried to soothe my irritability by taking deep, steady breaths. I needed to focus to prevent another fall that could have more serious consequences.

After a long uphill climb with some airy traverses on thin ledges, we and our porters stopped to rest and eat lunch on a ledge above a muddy pool near the river. I noticed that several of our porters dipped their food into the pool. Steven explained that the pool's water was salty. Salt was scarce in the jungle, so the local people used this resource. A wave of nausea swept over me, as I watched the porters eat food seasoned with muddy water.

Since my fall, some of the mud that caked my hands and clothes had dried and fallen off, but I was still filthy. I tried to remove the mud from my hands before touching my food. Using hand sanitizer did little more than grind dirt into my fingertips. "Don't worry about a little mud," Dan said. I was not reassured. Mud, especially mud rich in organic matter in the tropics, can include all sorts of pathogens. I was filthy, scraped, bruised, and still scared by my fall. I felt demoralized and incompetent. *Pull yourself together,* I commanded myself. I made myself drink water and eat a little, though everything tasted nasty.

After our break we crossed more rickety bridges of logs and branches. We were supposed to cross each bridge one at a time for safety reasons, but Ivan often ran up onto my heels, as I wobbled tentatively across slippery logs. Dan reminded Ivan to wait, until I had finished crossing. Once, Ivan impatiently splashed into one of the rivers and plunged across instead of waiting for his turn on the bridge. Dan said that he wanted us to use the bridges, which were safer than fording the swift rivers. Perhaps Ivan felt qualified to do things his own way because of his own experience in guiding hikes, being a captain in his country's army, and being 11 years older than Dan. I was impressed with Dan's quiet yet firm assertion of his authority as our expedition leader.

As the day progressed, Ivan calmed down. So did I. I regained my focus, my knees shook less, and I assumed my frightened crouch less often. We crossed a good-sized river to avoid a large landslide that had wiped out a section of our route. After our crossing, we noticed that local people had recently cut down lots of trees, leaving towering piles of slash, which we had to climb over. They had also built stick ladders up and down some of the steep, slippery slopes, a considerable amount of hard work on their part. Hiking was still like climbing through a continuous, untidy obstacle course, but the local people's recent trail improvements made our progress easier and safer.

The jungle became more luxuriant. Moss so green it seemed to glow covered roots, trunks, and branches like soft fur. This beautiful, primal Eden exceeded my wildest dreams of what the Papuan jungle would be like. Lushness suggested a gentler, kinder jungle, but it concealed new forms of treachery. Tangled mats of live roots and dead vegetation covered deep holes and trenches in the trail like pit traps into which an unwary hiker could fall and break a leg – or worse. Jumbled roots presented challenging obstacles that required climbing over or through. Now I better understood guide Kevin's dire warnings during the March trip about this treacherous terrain.

Carol Masheter climbing through jungle roots, photo by Dan Zokaites, July 8, 2012.

As I climbed over fallen trees, I could hear exotic bird calls. I had seen documentaries of Papua's birds of paradise and hoped to see some. The forest was so dense that I never saw the singing birds or any birds of paradise. Several times, as we clambered over steep forested hills and slogged through mud, the guys and I asked each other where all the animals were. Occasionally I found the tracks of what appeared to be a small canid. "A fox?" I asked Steven. "Yes, a fox," Steven replied. I could not tell whether he was confirming my guess or just humoring me. I never saw the little creature that made the tracks. Once I caught a glimpse of a furry rump and a naked tail disappearing into the undergrowth, probably a forest rat. Ironically the only animals I had gotten a good look at were villagers' pigs, chickens, and dogs during our first day in the forest.

As our porters passed us, I noticed that the women were collecting tendrils of pale green leaves that resembled water cress. Later that evening, I saw Raymond stirring the green leaves into a hot, soupy mixture of thread-like noodles and chunks of chicken for tonight's dinner. "What are those leaves called, Raymond?" I asked. He thought a moment and then said with a quick grin, "Indonesia salad, Miss Carol." I wondered whether Raymond was trying to find a name for these greens that was familiar to me, so I would be more willing to eat them.

At dinner, Dan urged us to eat lots, so we would have energy for tomorrow's hike. Nausea swept over me. As during previous meals, Jemmy reminded me to smile. I responded with an exaggerated grimace like an animal snarling. I hoped I was not over-using this joke with Jemmy. He meant well, after all. However, the last thing I felt like doing was smiling. I was soaked with sweat, muddy, and ached all over.

After dinner Dan summarized today's progress up and over a dozen steep ridges, the highest of which was about 12,500 feet elevation. According to Dan's altimeter, we had gained 5,000 vertical feet, lost 2,000 vertical feet, and covered 7.7 miles in nine hours. *Our hard day's work had given pathetic results,* I thought glumly, but Dan said we had made good progress today. We all brightened at this news.

The daily rain had held off, until we were under the dining tarp. This made keeping dry the interior of our sleeping tents easier than previous nights. However, keeping the mud out was another story. Today we had no nearby stream for bathing before crawling into our sleeping bags. Just outside my sleeping tent, I pulled off my disgusting, muddy clothes and boots, pulled on clean socks, base layer top, and bottom, which were already damp from the 100% humidity, and then stored my muddy clothes and boots under the tent's rain fly on top of my duffel, apart from where Dan and I would sleep. This arrangement was a compromise between keeping the inside of the sleeping tent as clean as possible, while having my mud clothes close at hand, off the muddy ground, and out of the rain.

July 9, 2012. I awoke, as the sky began to lighten before dawn. Dan's breathing was slow and regular, indicating that he was still asleep. Dan worked hard, often spending hours after the others had gone to their sleeping tents, organizing group gear, food, and fuel, conferring with the Indonesian guides, writing field notes about the day's travel, and sending dispatches of our progress to be posted on IMG's website. I did not want to deprive Dan of his well-earned rest. I eased out of my sleeping bag and crept out of our tent, careful not to wake him.

Outside, I watched fingers of clouds drifting among sharp, limestone ridges, toward which we would hike. I wondered whether we would climb above the forest and onto the high plateau today, where temperatures would be cooler and the terrain might be less rugged.

I felt sick. My belly had been bloated and sore from my usual irritable bowel symptoms for the past several days, but this was the first day I had felt ill. I took a Cipro (short for Ciprofloxacin), an antibiotic commonly used for GI bacterial infections, and clambered over a tangle of downed trees to the pit toilet. I felt marginally better after doing the necessary at the pit.

After breakfast and the daily argument between Jemmy and the porters, we left camp and labored up and down many steep ridges. The sun climbed higher in the sky. Heat and humidity rose, making us sweat like race horses. Dan paused ahead of me, as I plodded up a steep slope feeling strangely weak and dull. "You have slowed down a lot since this morning," he said in a flat, analytical tone. Hot shame burned my face. Embarrassed, I stammered, "I didn't realize that." "Let's give your climbing pack to a porter," Dan suggested. I feebly insisted that I could carry my own pack and would try to move faster. Dan replied that I was slowing the group. My heart sank. Reluctantly, I agreed to surrender my pack. "For the sake of the team," I mumbled, but I felt demoralized.

Negative self-talk flooded my thoughts. My slowness was a problem to our team. Now someone had to carry my pack for me. I did not want to be the weak little woman, the kind of woman that traditional mountaineers claimed had no place in the mountains. *What a loser I was,* I thought miserably.

Dan handed my yellow pack to a Papuan man shorter than me. The porter shot me a resentful look, swung my pack over his head on top of his regular load, and strode off on strong, bare feet. Tears of humiliation stung my eyes. I blinked them back and fell in grimly behind Dan, as we continued through the jungle. I felt terrible, both physically from being sick and emotionally for contributing to the porter's burden. I also felt bad for my fellow climbers. No one was carrying their packs.

I felt sicker as the day wore on, but Dan said I was moving faster. I had to admit that moving through the jungle without my pack was easier than when I was carrying it. We stopped to rest approximately every hour and a half. I lived for those rest stops. At each one I looked for the driest patch of mud and lay down. I felt as weak as a half-dead cat. *This would be my last big climb,* I resolved, *no more big mountains. I'm getting too old for such strenuous adventures.* I could not imagine ever feeling well again.

As I trudged sluggishly past some of our porters, who were sitting and resting on a little hill having their lunch, one of the women tugged my pant leg. She looked at me with an expression of earnest kindness and extended her cupped hands toward me. She held not her usual midday meal of yams roasted in last night's fire, but store-bought cookies, something she must have thought would appeal to me. I froze, stunned by her kindness and generosity. I tried to communicate my gratitude, murmuring simplified English and making gestures. "Thank you, you are so kind," I said, as I pressed my hands together as though in prayer. I realized that she probably did not understand what I was trying to say, but I floundered on. "I have a bad stomach," I said, with a sad expression. I rubbed my belly and mimed retching, "I can't eat, please keep your food," I cupped the woman's outstretched hands in my hands, and gently pushed them toward her. As I moved past her, my eyes filled with tears.

When I was a small child, my parents had taught my sister and me to give to charities and help others less fortunate than ourselves. One Sunday at our Methodist church, Reverend Washer had preached that true generosity was giving something you really needed. As a child and as an adult, I had always given out of my surplus. I could not think of a single time in my life, when I had given something I needed as much as this Papuan woman needed the food she had offered me. She had so little -- no shoes, maybe an extra pair of shorts, a few yams and a package of cookies. Today I felt a deep sense of gratitude and humility for this woman's example of true generosity and compassion. She had set a high standard that I was not sure I would ever match.

Papuan porters, photo by Pal Tande, July 9, 2012.

After lunch, we walked through patches of forest to more open, flat, treeless areas, where the ground was white clay. I wondered whether the absence of trees and most other plants was because the clay lacked enough organic material to sustain vegetation. We were on the plateau now, at about 12,000 feet elevation. Compared to climbing the many steep ridges in the jungle, the plateau seemed easy. Sometimes, when the trail was more or less level, and we were not struggling through knee-deep mud, or climbing over rocks, roots, or fallen trees, Dan told us that we could relax our focus and let our minds rest. The guys turned on their iPods, or we chatted and joked. One of the guys asked Steven whether we were past the mud. Steven's response was a high-pitched cackle with a manic edge.

Some of the plateau's flat areas were bogs of dark brown mud, where grass-like sedges grew and formed thick, wet mats of roots. I tried following Dan, stepping in his footsteps where the root mats had supported him. This method worked, since Dan outweighed me. I had found another way to avoid the strenuous work of wallowing in knee-deep mud, I thought happily. Just as I was beginning to trust the mats, my feet broke through, swallowing my boots to the knees and hobbling my feet. I flailed, fighting to maintain my balance, and barely avoided falling face down in the mud. Floundering to free myself drained my energy like a bath tub emptying itself of dirty water. Giving up meant I would remain as a permanent fixture in the bog, so I somehow found the energy to free my feet. I staggered on, panting like a sprinter after a race. I wiped mud and sweat from my face. Now we all knew why Steven had laughed when asked whether we were done with the mud.

Plateau bog, photo by Ivan Carrasco, July 9, 2012.

Since leaving Sugapa, my relationship with mud had been evolving. At first the mud mystified me. How could it be so slippery, so deep, so sticky, and so ever-present? Soon it infuriated me. Often when I took a step, the mud repelled my boot as though by some malevolent force, and I would fall. I would swear out of a mixture of surprise, anger, and pain. I hated how the mud clung to my boots and clothes like a diseased crust, how it grimed my hands and splattered my face, even splashed into my mouth, as I panted from the exertion of struggling through it. As the days passed, I discovered that hating the mud took too much energy, so I tried to determine which kinds of mud would support my weight or provide enough traction when climbing uphill. Just when I thought I was getting pretty good at reading the mud, it would pull a sly one and send me sprawling. I started growling like a wild beast instead of swearing, when I fell, in what I hoped was a less offensive way to express my frustration.

In the early evening we came to a bleak, treeless hill top. My weak-as-a-sick-cat state caught up with me. I sank to the ground like a deflating balloon, indifferent to the muddy ground. I lay there, browning out with fatigue, vaguely aware of activity around me. The porters were building a frame of branches for our dining tarp. I crawled a few feet out of their way and collapsed like a discarded rag doll.

Dan came over and grumbled that the porters had pitched our sleeping tent in a mud puddle. I lurched to my feet to help him move our tent to drier ground. Dan was right; our boots squished through boggy vegetation, as we relocated our tent. Clumsy with exhaustion, I was probably more hindrance than help.

I went in search of my duffel, so I could carry it to the sleeping tent and unpack my sleeping bag and pads. I passed a porter who was performing an improvised dance. Grinning broadly, he stamped his bare feet vigorously and made circles with his arms while holding two cooking pots. He looked festive with his elaborate Rasta braids bulging inside a large knitted cap, his red chest band, arm bands of woven plant fibers, and red and yellow striped shorts. His obvious joy was contagious. Being dance disabled, I joined the porter with a few jumping jacks, my version of dancing. The combination of being at 12,000 feet elevation and being sick made my head spin, so my "dance" was short lived.

Jemmy explained that the porter was celebrating, because we would get to Base Camp tomorrow. The day after tomorrow, while we climbed to the summit of Carstensz Pyramid, the porters would stay in a dry cave and rest. Nearing Base Camp was a good reason to celebrate. We all had been struggling through the jungle for days. Dale's and Roger's early departure from this trip, Dori's frightening fall, her head injury, saying a sad goodbye to Jason and the Schmidt family seemed like a long time ago. Now our jungle hike was about to end, and we would soon begin the climb, the reason we had come here.

The rain had started earlier than usual today, so we all were soaked, when we arrived in camp. I had found that wearing my rain jacket and rain pants kept out most of the rain, but even at

12,000 feet, I sweated under my rain gear, got very wet, and then became chilled. To avoid sweating so much, I had tried using my umbrella instead of my rain jacket, but I needed to use two trekking poles for balance, leaving no hand free to hold an umbrella. My umbrella was useful only in camp. Jemmy suggested that we take our wet clothes to the porter's tarp to dry near their fire. It was worth a try, so I changed into my dry base layer and dry socks then hung my rain jacket, muddy shirt, and muddy pants in thick clouds of acrid smoke.

Under the dining tarp I cautiously ate a modest serving of chicken stew. I had no appetite, but I chewed dutifully and swallowed carefully. Suddenly my mouth filled with too much saliva, and my belly cramped, sure signs that I was about to vomit. I jumped up from my camp stool and said hastily, "'Scuse me, I'm about to puke." Ivan looked at me with wide-eyed alarm and replied, "You're excused!" as I rushed past him. I ran up a faint trail then bent over, hands on knees, and waited for the revolting business to be over. Miraculously, the excessive salivating eased, and the nausea subsided. Just when I thought the moment had passed, the other end of my bowel went nuts. There was no time to find the pit toilet, but I managed to lurch into the brushes off the trail and drop my pants just in time.

I returned sheepishly to the dining tarp and quietly asked Dan, if I could speak with him privately. We went to the edge of camp out of earshot from the others. "I didn't make it to the pit toilet, but I got off the trail. I'm sorry," I confessed, dropping my gaze in embarrassment. Dan replied gently, "It's OK." Then he asked, "Is this usual for you?" I hesitated, before I replied, "I'm not sure. Sometimes my irritable bowel problems make me puke or have diarrhea, but no, this is not usual. I am concerned that I will be too weak for the climb and keep you guys from the summit."

To my horror, my eyes burned, my face convulsed into an involuntary grimace, and I began to cry. Dan put a brotherly arm around my shoulders and said, "You really want this summit, don't you?" "Hell, yes, I want it!" I blurted through my sobs, feeling like a complete fool. "Let's see how you feel tomorrow," he said quietly. I nodded vigorously, clawing away my tears. For a split second, I thought if I wiped them away fast enough, I could erase the mad rush from the dining tarp and then crying like a baby in front of Dan. Then reality flooded back in. I doubted I could recover from being sick soon enough to have a decent shot at the summit, but Dan's wait-and-see approach was the only game in town.

I was not the only one who was sick or having trouble. Earlier today I had noticed that Denis had rushed suddenly into the bushes. He had re-emerged, unusually quiet and pale, but he had soldiered on without complaint. Pal had been hoarse and coughing for days, yet he had denied being sick – until today. His tent mate, Dave, had caught his cold and was coughing a lot now. Dave was also experiencing back pain. He had joked about how the porters had laughed at his back stretches, but I knew he was worried. Back pain could be a show stopper for him. Ivan and Dan seemed to have avoided these troubles, but perhaps they were just better at concealing them and soldiering on. In fact, GI, respiratory, or back troubles, a sprain, or a fall could sideline any of us on summit day.

The others all had carried on without whining. No one was carrying their packs or comforting them through bouts of tears. My face burned with shame. As a child I had been raised not to cry or complain. As an adult I had seldom done either on my previous climbs. Now I felt like such a wimp. *This kind of thinking is not going to get me up the mountain,* I scolded myself. I squared my shoulders and went back to the dining tarp.

After dinner some of the Papuan boys gathered under our dining tarp out of the rain and watched us with shy curiosity. I had been reading my copy of "Why the Hell Bother?" by Ania Lichota about her experience of climbing the Seven Summits. First I, then Pal, showed the book's pictures to the boys. When we came to a picture of a Dani man wearing a penis gourd, they burst into big grins and called excitedly, "Dani! Dani!"

Soon a few men and women, perhaps the boys' parents, joined us. Pal and Ivan began to take photos. Ivan handed one of the boys a Kleenex to wipe the ever-present stream of mucus from his nose before having his picture taken. The boy swiped his nose and hurled the Kleenex away with a dramatic gesture, perhaps trying to cover his embarrassment. Some of the women were less willing to be photographed, but they watched with quiet pride, as the men and boys posed with grave dignity. Pal's and Ivan's ability to capture beautiful portraits impressed me, as did their generosity in sharing their photos with the rest of us later.

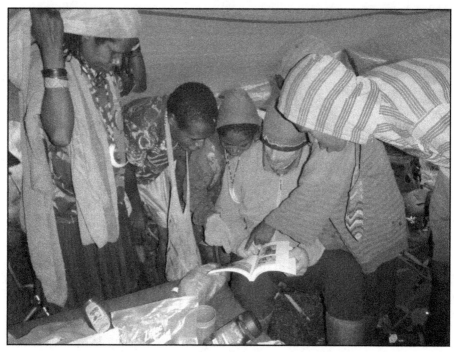

Porters and Pal Tande looking at pictures of the Seven Summits, photo by Carol Masheter, July 9, 2012.

The Warrior's Bow

July 10, 2012. Before breakfast I retrieved my hiking shirt and pants from the porters' shelter. My clothes were almost dry, but as I pulled them on, they stank so strongly of smoke that my nostrils stung. Part of me regretted leaving them near the smoky fire. The other part of me was glad to have clothes that were not soaking wet, even if they were not really dry.

At breakfast Dan scolded me for using tiny dabs of hand sanitizer. "Use more than that," he advised, "and keep it separate from your pit toilet supplies." I was running low on hand sanitizer and was trying to make it last through the rest of the trip, but I squirted a more generous gob into my grimy palm and smeared it between my fingers and under my nails like the TV surgeons, hoping it would penetrate several days' accumulation of dirt. Dan was trying to keep my gut problems from spreading further among the members of our group. *Too late,* I thought ruefully, remembering Denis' sudden dashes into the bushes yesterday. With my gimpy gut and my stinky clothes, I felt like Typhoid Mary.

After breakfast, I told Dan that I felt better and could carry my own climbing pack. He replied that I had done well without it yesterday, and he would like a porter to carry it again. Yesterday, I had not seen my pack all day and had been separated from my food and water. I had been too sick to eat, but I had needed more water.

Even at 12,000 feet elevation, it had been hot, and I had become dehydrated. I was disappointed that I was still not carrying my own pack, but I was relieved, because I could move more quickly without it. Dan said he would tell Jemmy to ask the porter to keep my pack closer to me today.

Dan also asked me to give him items from my duffel, so he could even out the weight of the porters' loads. I reluctantly gave him most of the Citrucel and Gentlelax I used to manage my irritable bowel symptoms. That was the last I saw of these items, until we returned to Timika. During the rest of the jungle hike I felt like a lion tamer without a whip or a chair in coping with my temperamental gut.

Ahead of us stretched a large, flat, treeless area covered with fine-grained white clay and much less vegetation. Sometimes the white clay was blessedly solid, a welcome change from the brown, knee-deep mud that held my boots in a vise-like grip, when I tried to free my feet. As in previous easier sections of our route, Dan said we could let our mental focus relax. In response I felt my stride lengthen and the tension in my body ease.

This easier hiking never lasted for long. Sometimes the innocent-looking white clay was as slick as grease. A lapse in focus, even for a fraction of a second, often caused a nasty fall onto the underlying hard-packed clay and rocks. A growing accumulation of bruises around my tailbone made me hobble painfully. Surely I looked ridiculous. I tried to find humor in the situation, but most of my energy went to trying to read the mud and avoiding more falls.

Ranks of weird trees stretched across the high plateau. Some looked like trees in a Dr. Seuss book – tall, naked trunks with live, spiky crowns and beards of dead fronds. We worked our way around thick patches of brush with tough, leathery leaves edged in little points, like holly leaves, only these points were sharper. Knee-high shrubs bloomed with orange, bell-shaped flowers that looked like they were made of heavy-gauge plastic. *Ironic that these flowers look artificial,* I thought, *here in one of the wildest, most remote places in the world.* The plateau landscape was angular, pointy, and straightforwardly tough in contrast to the deceptive softness of the jungle with its pretty green moss and concealed pits of mud.

The jungle was not finished with us. Steep, thickly forested ridges broke the relative flatness of the plateau and loomed between us and the distant limestone wall we were hiking toward. We struggled up and down the forested ridges, slipped into knee-deep mud holes, lunged out of them, and emerged onto another relatively flat area, only to enter another patch of jungle, and repeat the process.

The vegetation and formations of karst, a kind of very jagged limestone, became increasingly weird. We passed karst outcroppings that looked like the fossilized jaws of some giant, extinct beast from the Jurassic Period. We stopped for a short rest break near blocky towers of karst that resembled the ruins of ancient temples. As we continued on, I tried to spot something in the distance that resembled pictures of Carstensz Pyramid that I had seen online, but nothing looked familiar. We could have been on an alien planet in another galaxy.

Around midday during a pause in the rain, we found relatively dry, high ground and stopped for lunch. One of the porters shinnied up the tall trunk of a Dr. Seuss tree, his strong, bare feet gripping the trunk like the powerful talons of a raptor. He used his machete to cut loose a brown, prickly, oblong fruit larger than an American football. Back on the ground, he hacked open the fruit. Inside looked like a spoiled pineapple, fibrous and brown. Some of the guys tried a piece. None of them had much to say about it, so I reckoned it wasn't very good and declined a taste. Still, our porters' ability to find wild food in the jungle was impressive.

When Jemmy brought some of the porters' roasted yams for us to try, I felt a little braver and accepted a piece. I broke off the brittle, charcoal-roasted shell and tentatively tasted the soft, whitish inside. It wasn't bad – bland and starchy, a bit like a baked potato. Some of the guys were eating yellow yams and raving about how good they were, so I asked for some. It was sweet and flavorful, like the yams I ate at home. I waved to a group of our porters, who were sitting as a group nearby, grinned, pointed at the piece of yellow yam, and rubbed my belly. They grinned back. I asked for another piece of yellow yam, ate a little more, and then made myself stop. Though I was feeling better, I didn't want to push my luck.

Dan gave us the three-minute signal – time to put away snacks and water, stand up, shoulder our packs, and resume walking. We waded through more white mud and brown mud, and scrambled over jagged karst covered with a slippery pelt of emerald-green moss. We forded rivers now, as there were no nearby trees for making bridges. Fortunately, the rivers were smaller than those we had crossed in the jungle, but our crossings often were complicated by having to step on thin fins of karst. These fins seemed as sharp as knives, unless they were covered with moss; then they were as slick as grease. We needed to concentrate on each foot placement in this kind of terrain.

Carol Masheter scrambling over moss-covered karst at a stream crossing followed by Denis Verrette, Pal Tande, Dave Mauro, Ivan Carrasco, Jemmy Makasala, and Raymond Rengkung, photo by Dan Zokaites, July 10, 2012.

We passed several sink holes, some quite visible and deep, others choked with vegetation, their depths hidden. "A caver's paradise," Dan murmured, his eyes sparkling with an explorer's appetite for adventure. I usually liked caves but not today. The sink holes looked menacing, like gaping mouths ready to snatch unwary passers-by, snapping limbs and bashing heads. Images from Dori's terrifying fall flashed through my mind. *No more falls,* I told myself firmly. *Stay focused, place each foot carefully.*

We came to a steep hillside with nearly vertical slabs of limestone, which we needed to climb. Dan asked whether anyone wanted to be belayed with a rope. A fall here would be several dozen feet and could have serious consequences. We all shook our heads, but my fear of heights bubbled up, and my heart beat faster with anxiety. Once we started climbing, the steep limestone was not as difficult as it looked. It was no harder than off-rope climbing I had done back home. The guys and I took turns grasping each other's wrists and helping each other up some of the ledges. Denis did particularly well with the climbing and politely refused my out-stretched hand. Dan reminded Ivan to pull the hood of his rain jacket over his head, as the rain came down harder. I smiled to myself, *Dan is always looking after us like the good guide he is.*

Past the steep ledges, we picked our way between parallel fins of gray karst. The sharp fins were difficult to walk on, but the deep mud between them, often hidden by soft greenery, was more treacherous. Sometimes I could hear Dave, Pal, Ivan, and Denis behind me breathing hard with effort, and fatigue showed in their faces during our short rest breaks, but they stayed positive. They complimented my progress through rough terrain. Ivan said that I was fitter than his wife, who was half my age. Pal told me that I looked better today and was getting my color back. This was reassuring news, especially coming from a physician like Pal.

Climbing steep limestone fins,
photo by Dan Zokaites, July 10, 2012.

The guys and I helped each other stay positive with shared humor. Most mountaineering teams of which I have been a member develop their own inside jokes. Our team was no exception, even after the upset due to the early departure of more than half our group. Perhaps the early troubles had helped bond those of us who remained. Or perhaps shared humor was one of the ways we bonded. Like the chicken and the egg, I was not sure which came first. Early in our jungle hike, Dave had pressed his iPod to each of our ears, so we could hear his recording of Mr. T's "quit yo jibba jabba." My first response was to stare at Dave blankly, since I didn't know Mr. T. Dave's usual broad grin had flagged with disappointment. I felt like an old fogy for knowing so little about today's music. However, Dave was patient with my ignorance, and I soon got the joke. As the days passed, "quit yo jibba jabba" became one of our favorite refrains, especially when the going got tough.

Another shared joke was "the Movement," instigated by Ivan. No, it's not what you're thinking. Gut problems were never funny on this trip. The Movement referred to our insistence that "real" Carstensz Pyramid climbers approached the mountain the "pure" way, via the jungle hike. "We don't need no stinkin' helicopter or Mine road," we hooted. We joked about starting a movement to ban helicopter and road access to the peak. We tried to come up with a better name, but we failed. "The Movement" was the name that stuck.

The mud situation became so ridiculous, the guys and I started began to riff on it. "Here's mud in your eye!" "Your name is Mudd!" "Become One with the Mud!" "How many names for mud do the Papuans have?" We started to count the kinds we had encountered: brown mud, black mud, yellow mud, tan mud, white mud; mud to our ankles, mud to our knees, mud to our mid thighs; mud that crept over the tops of our knee-high boots and sneaked down into our socks; thick, sticky mud that grabbed our boots and yanked them off our feet; mud slicker than grease that repelled our feet as though by black magic; thin, watery mud that splashed in our face from the guy's boots in front of us; mud that splashed in our face from our own boots; mud that splashed our backsides

from the guy's boots behind us; mud that caked our boots, mud
that coated our pants to the crotch, mud that splattered our shirts
and ball caps; mud that hung from roots and branches in the trail;
mud that got into our food and gritted between our teeth; mud that
grabbed one leg of our camp stools, causing us to topple into more
mud; mud that squished between our toes on river banks when we
splashed ourselves clean; mud that crept into our tents at night,
while we were sleeping. "We're in the Land of 50,000 Kinds of
Mud," I shouted to my companions, as we tramped through yet
more mud. They hooted in merry agreement.

We climbed up a line of hills that overlooked a large, distant
lake. I could make out little upside down V's in the lake's dark
surface. The V's were probably caused by water birds, perhaps
ducks or geese, swimming rapidly away from us. Later as we
passed another distant lake, I saw more little V's moving away.
Then it struck me. *Papuans probably come here to hunt. No
wonder the birds are swimming away as fast as they can. Hunting
could also explain why we had seen no animals in this remote
jungle.*

Later in the day, we started up the stony New Zealand Pass,
pioneered by Philip Temple from New Zealand in 1962. Finally,
we were past the mud and on rocky ground. Some of the guys
wanted to change into their mountain boots, but Dan advised,
"Keep your mountain boots dry and free of mud for summit day."
I too had wanted to change into my mountain boots for better
footing on the rock, but I was pleasantly surprised that my mud
boots gripped the rock better than I had expected, and my feet slid
inside them less than our first days of hiking. As Dan predicted,
we still had to climb through some patches of deep, slick mud, so
mud boots were the better choice for now.

The rain came down harder, and the temperature dropped, as
we gained altitude. I shivered in my soaked rain jacket and rain
pants. I hoped the route would remain free of slick ice. Most
of the guys used their umbrellas to keep the rain off their heads,
but I still preferred using two hiking poles for balance, leaving no
free hand to carry an umbrella. We passed a group of our porters
crouching in a group near a limestone wall for a rest break. Some

had wrapped themselves in their thin capes, which were soaked through. They stared stoically into the cold rain, as we passed them. I tried to thank them for their hard work, but I doubted that they understood me. Dave murmured something to Dan about their obvious discomfort, barefoot and dressed only in soaked shorts and T-shirts. Dan replied, "Suck it up, Snowflake," implying that this mountain did not care about anyone's hardships, the porters' or ours.

New Zealand Pass is actually a series of rocky saddles, each higher than the last. On the way up to the first saddle, Ivan found a split bamboo bow at least three feet long. Its bowstring of woven plant fibers had been attached to each end of the bow with elaborate weavings of thin strips of split bamboo. It was a magnificent work of handcrafted weaponry. Ivan started to take the bow as a souvenir. No doubt, as a captain in his country's army, the weapon had special significance to him. Some of us thought it might belong to one of the porters, and we should leave it where Ivan found it. As Ivan put it back, I looked at it longingly. It was just the sort of authentic souvenir I wanted from this trip. However, leaving it for its owner to recover was the right thing to do. Perhaps I could buy a similar bow from one of the porters after our summit climb.

A long, upward traverse took us over the highest saddle at 14,600 feet elevation. On the other side we could see three large, green lakes in a valley of glacier-polished stone. Tears of joy leaked from my eyes. I was so glad to have gotten this far after so many difficulties.

We made our way down a long, winding route of steep chutes and loose rock, to the far shore of the middle lake, where porters would set up the blue dining tarp and our sleeping tents. Nearing camp I spotted a large brown bird with a reddish beak and feet, the first wild bird I have seen up close in Papua. Limestone crags beyond our camp seemed to play hide and seek in curtains of blowing mist. Base Camp was a wonderful sight after only about six hours of hiking, a short day for us. Even better, the early dinner of macaroni and cheese, something I normally do not like, was the first food that tasted good to me, since I had gotten sick.

Over dinner, Dan briefed us on what to wear and what to bring in our packs for tomorrow's climb to the summit. We would get up at 3:30 a.m., have a light breakfast, and start moving at 4:30 a.m. The early start and climbing in the dark by the light from our headlamps was a reasonable trade for a better chance of climbing before the daily rain started. Back in my sleeping tent, I changed into some of my climbing clothes, which I had kept clean and dry in a waterproof compression sack, to get a head start on preparation for our climb. I slid into my sleeping bag wearing a base layer top, a red wind-resistant, winter bicycling top, light-weight glacier pants, and liner socks.

I could not sleep much, due to a mixture of excitement and anxiety. I was too warm, so I took off the red top and added it to the jackets under my head that served as a pillow. Before midnight, I left the tent to find the pit toilet. I noticed a few stars in the night sky, a good sign that the rain clouds were breaking up. I hoped we could climb at least to the top of the limestone wall, before the daily rain began. Better yet would be finishing our climb and returning to Base Camp before the deluge. That might be too much to hope for, but a woman could dream….

Dream I did. Weird images scurried around inside my head like crazed mice. One dream started with something about the summit climb, then shifted to climbing through the studs of a building under construction, then changed to hiding from terrorists in a strange hotel in a strange city. *It must be the altitude,* I reasoned, when I woke up at 1 a.m.. I had sometimes experienced strange dreams when sleeping at high altitude, though usually at elevations above 17,000 feet. The dream, though odd, was reassuring, as it meant that I had gotten some high quality sleep.

Ribbons of Light

July 11, 2012. It was 3:30 a.m., time to get up. I didn't feel great, but I felt better than I had the last several days. I hoped it was good enough to get me to the summit safely without delaying the rest of the team.

An hour earlier Dan had dressed and went to meet with the Indonesian guides. Now, as I dressed, each of my exhaled breaths hung in the air, as I pulled on layers of clothing against the cold: a fleece ski hat, a grid-fleece pullover, a soft-shell jacket with a hood, and rain pants with full-length leg zippers. I rechecked the contents of my climbing pack: synthetic-filled parka, rain jacket with hood, helmet, harness with ascender and safety, both one-liter bottles full of water, light-weight ice-climbing gloves, and snacks for a long day of climbing. I pulled on a pair of medium-weight wool socks over my liner socks then my mountain boots. I stuffed my Petzl belay gloves into my pocket.

Outside the tent, ice crystals sparkled on the vegetation. Stars spangled the night sky. I smiled. I felt like a space walker, picking my way through a galaxy, stars above me, and stars below me. On a more pragmatic note, the clear, starry sky promised a dry start to our climb.

Under the dining tarp, I balanced my rump on a three-legged camp stool and hunched over a bowl of muesli and reconstituted powdered milk. Dark shapes with headlamps emerged Cyclops-like from the night and joined me. We didn't talk much, but I could feel the electricity of shared anticipation. After all the challenges and uncertainties -- Ivan's visa troubles, delayed flights to Sugapa, injuries and evacuations, porter arguments, back pain, GI bugs, respiratory troubles, days of toiling up and down steep muddy ridges through the jungle and across the plateau, this was it. It was show time!

Dan changed his mind about having us wear our rain pants. Now he suggested that we take them off. After we had stripped off and packed away our rain pants, we shouldered our packs and headed out of camp. I was cold, but it was better to start a bit too chilly, as the effort of climbing would soon warm me. We wove our way through limestone boulders and wound up slopes of scree and talus. After days of wearing my mud boots, I felt slow and clumsy in my mountain boots. Even while following the small circle of light from my headlamp, I tripped a couple of times over rocks I did not see. Each time I staggered, caught my balance, and did not fall. We picked our way up and over several ridges of limestone.

In about an hour, we reached a gray mass that reared up in the pre-dawn darkness. We scrambled up a boulder-strewn cleft to where it pinched to a narrow alley between steep walls. Our approach was over, and we were about to begin climbing nearly 2000 vertical feet. I found a good boulder to sit on and worked my harness leg loops over my boots, tightened and double backed the waist strap, adjusted the leg loops, and made sure my ascender and safety carabiner were ready to clip onto the fixed line. I transferred my headlamp to my climbing helmet, centered the helmet on my head, and tightened the chin strap. I shook my head gently to be sure the helmet was snug without being too tight. Then I sat hunched against the cold.

While I waited for the others to get ready, I traced the loose end of the fixed line with the beam of my headlamp up the wall. The wall looked steep. Self-doubt bubbled up like toxic waste. *Would I be skilled enough to climb this wall? Would my mountain boots stick to the steep limestone? Would my Petzl belay gloves would be warm enough yet sensitive enough for me to find and grip hand holds? Would I be strong enough to haul myself hand-over-hand across the Tyrolean traverse on the summit ridge? Or, if the Tyrolean traverse were not useable, would I be able to down climb the steep gap and then climb up a rope at least 60 vertical feet on the other side using wrap prusiks as stirrups for my feet? Could I keep up with my team mates? Would my gut behave today, or would I join the brown underwear club?* An involuntary shudder swept through my body, especially at this last appalling thought.

Stop it! I ordered myself. *You have prepared well for this climb. You have trained hard. You can do this!*

Steven, our lead Indonesian guide, had already disappeared up the rope into the darkness, while we were putting on our climbing gear. Even after talking back to my self-doubt, I was scared. I did not want to go first. Denis stood up, indicating he would go. He clipped his ascender and safety onto the fixed line. Dan advised him step up onto an upward sloping, natural ramp several inches wide about three feet up the wall, shuffle along the ramp to climber's right perhaps 15 feet to where the face was less steep, and then begin climbing straight up from there. I watched Denis, until he slowly disappeared behind a bulge in the wall. *That didn't look too hard,* I thought, my self-doubt easing a little.

Best to get it over with, I coached myself. I went next. I traversed the starting ledge slowly and deliberately, pushing my ascender up the fixed line and pulling its loose end through, taking up the slack, to where Denis had begun climbing up. I slid my ascender and safety up the line with my right hand as far as I could reach, bent my knee and found a foothold for my right foot up the wall, then for my left foot, straightened my legs and stood tall, sliding my ascender and safety up the line. I repeated these moves, inch-worming up the wall. I sometimes fumbled the loose end of the fixed line in the dark. I felt awkward and self-conscious. I imagined that the guys behind me were critiquing my clumsy technique. After three or four moves, I found a rhythm and made smoother progress. The climb was steep, but the hand holds and foot holds were generous and solid. The rock was sharp enough to cut my hands to ribbons had I not been wearing leather gloves.   That sharpness provided plenty of friction, so my hands and feet did not slip.

I came to a nearly vertical place, where the fixed line's mantle was completely torn through to the core.   To my relief, my ascender slid past the damaged mantle without jamming, and the naked core held my weight. Some of the guys called out words of encouragement. The climb was easier than I had expected. My confidence increased a little. *Maybe I can do this climb after all.*

I climbed perhaps 30 to 40 vertical feet, when the wall became less steep. This became a pattern. We would climb a nearly vertical pitch, followed by a less steep slope, then another steeper pitch. The wall was like a giant staircase with downward slanting steps. On each step, we could regroup, adjust our clothing layers, and drink. The exertion of climbing the first steep section made me too warm, so I shed my soft-shell jacket.   Some of the guys passed me, while I stuffed the jacket into my pack.

As we climbed the steep sections, our metal ascenders and carabiners clinked against the wall. Their soft, clear notes were the only sounds except for the steady huff and puff of our breathing. I began to feel a sense of peace and growing confidence. All was going well.

Suddenly a rock whizzed past my left ear, then another crashed into the wall just above me. A third rock struck my helmet hard enough to jerk my head sharply downward toward my right shoulder. The guys climbing above me had knocked off several good sized rocks. Dan shouted at them to be more careful. Climbers customarily shout "Rock!" as a warning, when loose rock falls, but for some reason this was not happening today. At our next gathering place, I went to the front of the line behind Steven to avoid being hit by more falling rocks. I could hear the guys knocking more rocks loose below me, as we moved up the next steep section. Dan yelled that the rock fall was not acceptable.   I hoped no one would get nailed more seriously than I had just been. We were so close to accomplishing what we had come here to do, an accident now would be a terrible disappointment in addition to the difficulties and dangers of self-rescue from this isolated place.

While climbing up one of the less steep steps at perhaps a 30-degree angle, I suddenly face planted on what looked like damp clay. The right side of my face stung, where it had smacked into the hard ground. I had slipped and fallen on verglas, a transparent shell of very slick ice coating the clay. *Just as my confidence was increasing, Carstensz Pyramid tricked me,* I smiled wryly to myself. I got to my feet and made a mental note to be more careful.

On another less steep section, we picked our way through huge boulders of fallen limestone that loomed above us like dinosaurs. I hoped none of them would cut loose and come crashing down on us. *Put it out of your mind and climb,* I ordered myself. *Don't trust any holds without testing them first – carefully.* I did not want to knock anything loose, especially one of those boulders, onto those below me.

A strange, smoky-orange light glowed in the sky to climber's right. I asked Dan about it. He said it was lights from the Freeport Mine. We were that close. As we climbed higher, we could see into the Mine's huge terraced pit. The terraces glowed with curving ribbons of red and pale yellow, the tail lights and head lights of ore trucks four stories tall grinding up and down gravel roads within the pit. From what I knew about the Mine -- the destruction of nearby forest and pollution of rivers, exploitation of local people, recent strikes and violence – I hated it. However, the ribbons of light gave the Mine a strange, hellish beauty.

A thin strip of orange glowed in the east. Dawn was coming sooner than I had expected. During past climbs, the predawn hours had often seemed very long and difficult. My heart quickened with the promise of more light and warmth from the rising sun. Soon we would be able to enjoy more of the view, as we climbed up the wall of gray limestone.

On one of the lower angle slopes, Dan came up next to me and pointed above and to our left. There the Tyrolean traverse stretched across a gap in the ridge against the deep blue, pre-dawn sky. The gap looked like an unimpressive nick spanned by a black thread. I knew the gap was about 60 feet deep, at least that wide, and bridged by thick ropes. It looked tiny from here, which meant we still had a lot of climbing to do. It was time to get back to work. I looked down, found my next footholds, and stepped up.

Soon I had to pee, a good sign that I was well hydrated but an annoying distraction. When we reached a large, less steeply angled step, Steven pointed to climber's left as a safe place for me to find a "ladies room." I unclipped from the fixed line and traversed carefully across angle-of-repose talus. I found a place among boulders about 50 yards from the guys to use my pee funnel in relative privacy and get the job done without loosening and lowering my harness. More experienced climbers than I have forgotten to tighten a loosened harness and have fallen to their death. Now I could focus on climbing without the distraction of a full bladder.

On some of the steeper sections of the wall, the hand holds and foot holds were thin. I could grip my ascender on the fixed line for one hand hold and palm bulges in the wall with my other hand. My feet in their bulky, stiff mountain boots were a bigger concern. However, I had been able to make them stick on relatively smooth quartzite during my climb of the West Slabs on Mount Olympus in Utah a few weeks before this trip. The Carstensz Pyramid wall was steeper than the quartzite of the West Slabs, but the limestone was more textured and provided more friction. I was able to make my feet stick, even with very little rubber on my boots' stiff toes pressed onto the wall.

Sometimes Dan told me I was taking the hard way and pointed to a less steep or less smooth line to my right or left. I had been so focused on climbing that I had not noticed the easier line off to one side. *Easy is good*, I chuckled to myself. *There would be plenty of hard stuff ahead.*

Carol Masheter nearing the top of the limestone wall, Jemmy Makasala watching just ahead of her, photo by Pal Tande, July 11, 2012.

Flying Upside Down

Sooner than I expected, we gained the top of the ridge. Dan praised our progress and our pace. As pleasing as this was, after years of mountaineering, especially at high altitude, I had learned to never assume my companions and I would reach the summit, until we actually touched the top, no matter how close we might be. Weather could deteriorate, a team member could fall or experience serious altitude sickness, part of the route might be impassable – all situations that could force us to turn back short of the summit, even after climbing this far. However, Dan's praise suggested that we had a good chance. Our Indonesian guides went ahead, as we scrambled over and around towering pinnacles on the jagged ridge. Some places were exposed with steep drops of hundreds of feet. *Don't get over confident,* I reminded myself. *Make sure each step is solid.*

As the sun rose, its light transmuted the cold, gray limestone into warm gold. The sunlit rock sparkled as though it were encrusted in tiny diamonds. *Now I believe in alchemy,* I thought. *I must get a sample of this dazzling rock to take home.* It took me perhaps half a minute to realize that the crystals were frozen mist. *Another lesson in impermanence,* I smiled to myself. The next best thing to collecting a sample would have been taking a photo, but my camera had gotten too wet from yesterday's rain and had stopped working. I had to settle for a mental photograph of being surrounded by golden rock sparkling with diamond dust. I concentrated hard to fix these other-worldly images in my mind. People have asked me again and again why I climb. Experiencing such beauty is one of many reasons.

Clouds floating among the ridge's crags turned orange, then peach, then gold, their backlit edges aflame. Curtains of mist blew over the jagged ridge in front of us, streaming through its gaps like Pashmina wool through a giant comb, an enchanting and oddly familiar sight. Then I remembered seeing videos on the Internet of the mist streaming over the ridge just like this. *We are really here!*

We scrambled up and down giant teeth that formed the ridge. Again, I was struck by how sharp and jagged the limestone was, sharper than any other rock I had known. Moving along the ridge was not as hard work as climbing up the steep wall, but it required just as much focus. Taking a catastrophic fall was still a very real risk. Our progress was slow and careful.

Ahead the Tyrolean traverse came into view, four beefy ropes and a steel cable spanning a wide gap between rocky horns. From where I stood, I could not see the bottom. Jemmy and Raymond had already traversed the gap and were waiting on the far side. I was among first climbers to arrive at the gap, but I let the guys go before me, partly to give them a chance to be ahead of me -- they had followed me patiently for days through the jungle -- and partly to pull myself together for the scary business of crossing that airy gap.

I sat crouched in the rocks and went through my personal care tasks. I was not thirsty, but my mouth was dry, probably from the exertion and anxiety of the climb. I drank a little water then drank some more. I was not hungry, but I ate a few Clif Bloks. Past experience had taught me that if I waited until I was hungry during a cold, high climb, I had waited too long, and my moves would be weak and clumsy. Blowing mist snatched away the precious, thin layer of body heat my clothing had trapped. I dug my soft-shell jacket out of my pack and pulled it on, my chilled fingers fumbling with the zipper. I tugged the hood over my climbing helmet to keep the freezing mist off my neck and head.

Shivering in the rocks, I watched Denis clip onto the ropes and cable with help from Dan and Steven. Dan gave Denis the signal to start across the gap. Denis eased down a cleft in the jagged rock feet first and disappeared. When I next saw him, he was hanging below the ropes and cable, facing the sky, his head pointed toward the far end of the gap, his hands grasping the ropes, his legs hooked over them pirate-style. *How did Denis turn himself 180 degrees without slamming into the rocks?* I wondered. I wished I had seen that transition, so I would know the best way to make it, but I had not wanted to be in the way on the cramped edge of the gap, while Dan and Steven helped Denis clip in. Dan shouted at Denis to take his legs off the ropes and let them hang, but he either did not hear or did not understand. He pulled himself across laboriously, slowing even more on the uphill half of the wide U the ropes and cable made across the gap.

At last Denis' helmet neared the far end of the gap. I watched carefully, hoping to learn from Denis' experience. Denis had to unhook his legs from the ropes, turn his body 180 degrees, so he faced the far wall, and find holds for his hands and feet to climb up the last bit. Denis flailed in several attempts to climb the wall. Raymond and Jemmy finally grabbed him, hauled him up to a safe landing place, and detached him from the ropes and cable, so he could move up the ridge away from the gap. Then it was the next guy's turn to make the crossing.

I watched each team member clip onto the traverse, then cross, and detach. During the crossing, letting their legs hang seemed to work better than hooking them over the ropes. They could hand-over-hand across the gap faster and apparently with less effort. However, when I had practiced this method back home, letting my legs hang had put painful pressure on my lower back. I would just have to see what happened today, when it was my turn. I studied where each of the guys placed his feet on the smooth, steep wall at the far end of the traverse and how they positioned their bodies, so Jemmy and Raymond could help them detach from the ropes and cable.

Everyone except Dan and Steven had gone across. It was my turn. I was scared but eager to get moving and get it done. I took deep, steady breaths to keep my anxiety at a manageable level. I tightened my helmet chin strap, my pack's shoulder straps, chest strap, and hip strap. I felt a bit like Jody Foster's character, Eleanor Arroway, in the movie, "Contact," as she was strapped into an alien travel machine: scared, excited, focused, determined.

I inched carefully to the edge of the gap and positioned myself in a reclining posture, so Dan could clip my harness carabiner onto the four ropes, and Steven could clip my Purcell prusik onto the cable. The guides' methodical instructions and assistance were calming. I squeezed both carabiners to be sure they were locked. My brow relaxed. I had not realized it had been furrowed with anxious concentration.

At Dan's signal, I lowered myself down steep rocks into the gap using my hands and feet as brakes. When I felt the ropes take my weight, I made the 180-degree turn, so the top of my head faced the far side of the traverse, and I was facing skyward.

Carol Masheter crossing the Tyrolean traverse in freezing mist, photo by Dan Zokaites, July 11, 2012.

Half of me wanted to look over my shoulder down into the gap below. The other half was too scared to look. The scared half won. Concentrating on the sky above, a hole opened in the blowing mist showing clear, blue sky. *A good sign,* I thought. Manic glee raced through my body, as I hand-over-handed across the gap. A crazy, joyous thought raced through my brain, *I was flying upside down!*

Carol Masheter crossing the Tyrolean traverse after a hole opened in the mist, photo by Denis Verrettte, July 11, 2012.

The first half of the traverse seemed easy, which was not surprising, since it was downhill. Pulling myself uphill on the second half was harder work. I kept stopping and looking over my shoulder to gauge my progress and to avoid banging my head on the far wall. Puffing hard, I forced my hands and arms, now weakening with fatigue, to keep going. Then I was there, at the far end of the gap. Over my noisy gasps for air, I was vaguely aware of the guys' cheers.

It was not over yet. Detaching from the traverse had looked tricky for my team mates. Watching the guys go before me had given me ideas for the more promising places for my hands and feet on the smooth rock wall. It was still difficult. During my first attempts, my feet slipped. I kept trying, until I managed to find tiny holds and pull myself onto the top of the horn. While I clutched the rock like a lizard, feeling a bit ridiculous, Raymond and Jemmy seemed to take a long time to detach my locked carabiners from the ropes and cable. Free at last, I thanked them with a rush of breath I had been holding. Triumph and relief swept over me like a tidal wave. *I had done the Tyrolean traverse! We all had!* Dan later told us that some climbers got as far as that traverse and freaked out. They turned back without summiting.

Now all we had to do was climb the ridge to the summit. My thoughts started to race ahead. *Maybe there is another easier way down from the summit,* I hoped. *Snap out of it!* I scolded myself. *Focus on what you need to do right now! Get to the summit. Then think about getting down.*

All my team mates had moved ahead on the ridge, except for Dan, Steven, and me. I wanted to hurry and catch up with the others, but I also wanted to savor this climb, the last of my Seven Summits. My emotions threatened to boil over. I was about to fulfill a dream that had taken five and a half years. I had experienced strenuous challenges, moments of intense joy and satisfaction as well as frustration, disappointment, and fear. These extremes felt curiously familiar. I had experienced them, as I neared the summit of Everest a little over four years before this climb. Now I was about to become the oldest woman in the world to complete the Seven Summits including Carstensz Pyramid.

As we worked our way up the ridge, we encountered another gap. It was much smaller than one spanned by the Tyrolean traverse, perhaps 10 feet across and 10 or 15 feet deep, but to me it was more terrifying. For this smaller gap the guides suggested that each of us wrap the fixed line around our trailing arm and then, leaning down and outward, take a long step, or in my case, a controlled fall, across the gap to its far wall. I had used the arm-wrap method on previous climbs, but I had never had to fall like this. I watched the guys ahead of me for hints on how it could be done safely. My careful observation turned to horror, as Dave lost his footing and fell into the gap. His Purcell prusik, attached to the fixed line spanning the gap, caught him. He hung there like a spider for what seemed like a long time. Somehow Dave got across the gap. I was too busy trying to remember how to breathe to take in the details of how he did this.

Then it was my turn. I felt sick. Dave's fall had unnerved me. I wrapped the fixed line around my left arm and turned first one way, then the other, trying to find a way to step across the gap without falling. Nothing I tried felt safe. I felt off balance, at risk of taking a twisting fall into the gap, and slamming into the opposite wall. With some patient coaching from Dan, I finally fell across the gap and landed clumsily like a newly fledged sparrow landing from its first flight.

We worked our way up the ridge toward the summit. As we scrambled over crags and around pinnacles, we crossed several patches of crusty snow. I made sure each step was solid, especially where the snow patches sloped downward above a drop off. We were getting close to the summit. *Falling now would be too ironic*, I reminded myself.

Ahead, rocky ledges, each about five to ten feet high, led to a point above which there was no more up. I could see an ice axe silhouetted against the sky. *That must be the summit,* I hoped cautiously. It seemed too good to be true. My hope flickered tentatively then flared into a super nova. A crazy little chant started inside my head. *I'm gonna do this, it's for real!* I felt disoriented, even dizzy. *Was it the altitude? Fatigue? The chaos of emotions I'm experiencing?* I shook my head to clear it. *Quit yo jibba jabba, I'm doing this!* The guys ahead were sitting along the last bit of ridge leading to the ice axe. Seeing them there, marking the way like lights on a runway, helped ease my disorientation. Later, I learned that they had agreed to stop and let me be first to touch the true summit, a true act of collective gallantry.

Carol Masheter nearing the summit,
photo by Pal Tande, July 11, 2012.

The guys were calling eagerly to me to come up. *What splendid men they were!* I thought, giddy with joy. *I had waited, until I was nearly 66 years of age, before I met my prince charmings, all eight of them at once.* As I passed Dave, he asked me how old I was. His question seemed odd and out of place, but I dutifully mumbled, "65 years and nine months." As I took my final steps toward the pointy summit, I could hear Dave's voice behind me, narrating, "Ladies and gentlemen, you are about to see a world record being set. Carol Masheter, age 65 3/4, is about to summit the eighth of the Seven Summits, becoming the oldest woman in history to do so." Dave was making a video of my last steps to the top with his GoPro camera.

As I moved past the rest of my team mates, exchanging handshakes and fist bumps, a powerful undertow of emotions dragged my feet to an involuntary stop. Strange barks burst from my throat, as I sobbed and laughed at the same time, as though all the intense joy, sadness, and triumph in my life had crashed together and exploded like fireworks from my chest.

Carol Masheter laughing and crying at the same time near the summit of Carstensz Pyramid, Ivan Carrasco seated in foreground, Jemmy Makasala in black, photo by Pal Tande, July 11, 2012.

I had failed at work and at love, the two main tasks of adulthood according to Sigmund Freud. Yet, here I was, at nearly 66 years of age, setting a world record, surrounded by eight accomplished, younger men who had believed in me more than I had believed in myself. Ivan reached up from where he was sitting and took one of my hands, as I tried to regain my composure. *Get ahold of yourself,* I commanded myself. *Focus, don't blow it now.*

Just ahead I could see the battered ice axe leaning against the sky, a string of ragged prayer flags fluttering from its shaft. Slowly, savoring each step, I covered the last few feet. Dan, always our guide and watching out for our safety, intoned, "Just remember where you are. Take lots of photos, but be cognizant of where the edges are." Dave's voice rang out behind me, "Let's hear that howl!" referring to my customary summit howl. Time slowed to a crawl. It seemed to take forever to settle myself safely on a sharp bit of stone that was the true summit. I took a couple of slow, deep breaths. "AahhEEE!" I gasped, using our porters' all-purpose exclamation. Then I filled my lungs and belted out, "AAAHHHOOOO!!!!" See www.carolmasheter.com under Media for Dave's video.

Carol Masheter on the summit of Carstensz Pyramid, photo by Pal Tande, July 11, 2012.

Wide-eyed as a child, I took in the 360-degree view from my perch. Lower nearby peaks were wreathed in clouds. In the distance a dark blue blur was probably the Arafura Sea, perhaps from where Dutch explorer, Jan Carstensz, after whom this peak is named, had seen the snow-capped mountains of Papua nearly 400 years ago. Remnants of the rapidly receding glacier were visible over my left shoulder. Far below to my right was the high, stone valley where our Base Camp was, across that valley was the New Zealand Pass, then the boggy plateau, and the mountainous jungle beyond that had nearly defeated us.

I had sacrificed and struggled for years for this moment. I had trained hard for each climb. I had learned the appropriate skills and had climbed practice peaks. I had bought the best equipment and hired the best guides I could afford. I had retired from a job I enjoyed with people I liked to finish the Seven Summits. Now it was done. The sports writer Jolly Roger's quote, referring to the aging Seabiscuit's win of the Santa Anita Handicap, sang inside my head, "Oh that I have lived to see this day!"

Part of the view from the summit including the Freeport Mine, photo by Denis Verrette, July 11, 2012.

Brightest of Silver Linings

My time was up. Each of the guys was patiently waiting for a turn on the true summit. Dave posed holding pictures of his mother, his girlfriend, Lin, his sons, and a close friend, who had encouraged his climbing. Denis and Pal each had their proud moments on the summit with their respective national flag. Ivan had pictures taken, while he held the Dominican Republic flag and banners from his sponsors. I later learned that Ivan uploaded these pictures via satellite phone. The next day they made the front page of his country's largest newspaper. His country's Olympians then took that flag to London for the Summer Olympic Games of 2012.

After we each had our turn, we gathered just below the summit where we had enough room for a group photo. We crowded together, arms over each other's shoulders, grinning for the camera. Raymond graciously served as photographer, as no passing strangers were available for that role. Two weeks ago, we had been eight strangers from different countries and cultures. Today we were eight mountain bros and a mountain sister.

Group picture just below the summit, standing from left, Ivan Carrasco, Jemmy Makasala, Carol Masheter, Pal Tande, Dave Mauro, Denis Verrette; seated from left, Dan Zokaites, Steven Liwe, photo by Raymond Rengkung, July 11, 2012.

As we separated from our group pose, I stammered, "I can't think of eight more splendid men to have shared my last of the Seven Summits." My vision blurred with tears. I realized, *had the March trip not failed, I never would have met these guys and shared with them the jungle hike, the summit climb, the challenges and triumphs of the Brotherhood of the Rope. This is the brightest of silver linings.*

Dave took me aside and reminded me that I had agreed to help him scatter his deceased brother's ashes. We moved a little way from the others. Dave pulled out a small plastic bag from his pack. He opened the bag and let his late brother's ashes stream into the wind, as he murmured a few words of farewell. Without warning, my eyes blurred with tears again. I realized that Dave was crying, too. Without thinking about it, we leaned into a hug, sobbing together for a few moments. I cried for Dave's loss, thinking how terrible it must be to lose a brother. I also cried for my own losses. I thought of all the people that I had loved, who were now gone: my grandmother who had taught me the joys of gardening; my father who taught me how to change a tire, to cook a steak properly, and to always do my best; my aunt who spoiled my sister and me on weekends; my mother, who taught me to love nature and set high standard I sometimes failed to meet; all the men I had loved but had drifted out of my life with other women. Dan came over, his brow furrowed with concern. "What's going on?" he asked. I gave a brief explanation, trying to find the right balance between Dave's privacy and Dan's need to know.

I could hear the growl of ore trucks, as they labored up and down the winding gravel roads within the Freeport Mine pit. I resented their mechanical noise; it intruded on the wild, airy beauty of the summit. The upper terraces of the deep pit were visible, but the ribbons of light from the ore trucks' head lights and tail lights were gone. Full daylight had stripped the pit of its strange, pre-dawn beauty.

Clouds were thickening on the horizon, threatening rain. It was time to leave the summit and start back down. Dave and I each regained our composure. Everyone put away cameras and shouldered packs. Going down may be easier on the heart and lungs than climbing up, but climbers are often more tired than they realize after many hours of climbing, especially in the cold and at high altitude. As adrenalin from reaching the summit fades, fatigue creeps in, often unnoticed. Weather is more likely to deteriorate later in the day, when most descents occur, making the route more treacherous. For these reasons, mistakes, falls, and injuries are more likely to happen on the way down than on the way up. We could not relax our guard yet.

In addition to these challenges, I have one more, fear of heights. When I descend, I cannot avoid looking down. Looking down exacerbates my anxiety about falling. My inner whiner began to whimper, *I hate going down. I'm afraid I'll fall. I don't want to do this!* A silly hope resurfaced, *maybe we will go down a different way, an easier, less steep way. Don't be an idiot,* my rational self scolded. *If there were an easier route, we would have climbed up that way.* I countered my doubts by focusing on the positive, like the fact that each step down would bring us closer to Base Camp, where we would celebrate our successful climb over a hot meal. *Besides, I know how to descend,* I reminded myself. *I can do this.*

Descending the ridge, photo by Denis Verrette, July 11, 2012.

We worked our way down the ridge the same way we had come up. We all got better at moving down the rocky ledges, descending crusty patches of snow, and scrambling around jagged pinnacles. I was near the front of the team behind Steven and Jemmy. We scooted down a narrow chute on hands and feet, our rumps near the rock, as we approached the small gap that had frightened me during our ascent. My mouth went dry, as memories of Dave's fall flashed across my mind. When I scooted close enough to see the actual gap, I could see that I would be moving from the gap's lower side to its upper side and would not have to look down. *It doesn't look so bad,* I reassured myself.

The guys cheered, as I jumped across and scrambled up the other side. At the Tyrolean traverse, Steven crossed first, then

Denis. Jemmy helped me clip in. I launched myself head first, facing the sky, and briskly hand-over-handed myself across. The guys whooped and hollered their encouragement. Puffing like a steam engine, I was across sooner than I had expected. The landing and disengagement from the ropes and cable were easier on this side of the gap, because the wall was less steep, and hand holds and foot holds were more generous. Jemmy and I scurried down the ridge, following the fixed lines.

Again, sooner than I expected, we began the first of about 20 rappels down the wall. *No worries, I can do this,* I reminded myself, as Jemmy checked that I had set up my figure-eight rappel device properly. I backed down the first pitch carefully and slowly, as I was more accustomed to rappelling on two strands of rope instead of a single strand. The fixed line provided enough friction to descend safely, so I relaxed and let the rope slide through my rappel device, increasing my speed.

Carol Masheter rappelling down part of the limestone wall as Jemmy Makasala watches, photo by Ivan Carrasco, July 11, 2012.

When Jemmy saw that I was rappelling competently, he eased off on his surveillance and often descended in front of me. On one of the angled ledges, I accidently knocked loose a rock about the size of a loaf of bread that he had to dodge. I had been silently critical of the guys this morning, when they had knocked loose rocks down on me. Now I was the guilty party. I felt bad and apologized to Jemmy. He forgave me with a generous grin. We continued down the wall. A few of the descents included sections of free rappel, meaning I had to descend down the fixed line without my feet touching the wall, like a spider hanging by a strand of silk. I had done free rappels before back home. *No problem,* I reminded myself.

Sooner than I expected, I recognized the section of fixed line, where the mantel was worn through to the core. This was the first section we had climbed this morning, so it had to be our final rappel. Again, I passed the worn sections of rope without mishap. We were done with the fixed lines. Relief washed over me like a warm bath. Jemmy and I scrambled down and away from the wall out of the range of any falling rock. Looking back, I could see tiny figures far up the wall. *Was everything OK?* I wondered.

Jemmy said he was going on to Base Camp to start heating water for hot drinks. I glanced up at the threatening clouds. I really wanted to hurry back with Jemmy and avoid getting soaked in the impending rain. However, the guys had slowed their pace for me day after day in the jungle. They had waited for me to shuffle timidly across log bridges, when they wanted to rush ahead of me. They had not complained or criticized me, when Dan had a porter carry my pack. I would not desert my eight splendid men now. I took off my climbing harness and helmet, stowed them in my pack, and waited.

Within 20 or 30 minutes, Pal had descended the wall and joined me. He wanted to keep walking. My own impatience to get back to Base Camp overcame my more team-spirited impulses, and I followed him. However, guilt soon caught up. *This isn't right,* my better self reminded me. I called to Pal, "I'm going to wait for the others." Without looking back, he seemed to agree that we should wait, but he kept walking. My own legs would not stop. If anyone were ahead of me, I wanted to catch up and pass him. For better or worse, I was just as compulsive and competitive as the next person. I was not proud of this, but there it was. I called to Pal again; he agreed again to stop – without stopping. We repeated this crazy little call-and-response a few more times. Finally I made myself stop on a low mound with a good view of the wall that Pal and I had descended. Pal stopped perhaps 50 yards ahead. I wanted to join him, but if I started walking again, I suspected that he would also start walking. We waited separately. Perhaps we each needed our own space just then.

It began to rain. I shrugged off my pack, took out my rain pants and jacket, and pulled them on. Heavy drops splatted hard on my jacket hood. My rain gear kept me dry, but the wet, cold fabric pressed against my neck and back, sucking the heat from my body. Even near the Equator, it can be cold at 14,000 feet elevation, especially in rain just above the freezing point. I wondered how the guys were doing on the wall. They were out of sight now. *Was the rock becoming wet and slippery? Were the ropes providing enough friction for safe rappels? Was rain runoff turning the climb into a series of waterfalls?*

At last the guys came back into view, still high on the wall. I watched them make slow progress down. They paused on a ledge. I wondered why they had stopped and hoped again that they were OK. After perhaps five minutes, one started down very slowly. Others followed. This cycle repeated several times for the next 45 minutes. Later I learned that some of the guys had trouble with the rappels, as the rain had made the rock wall and the fixed lines very slippery. Some of them had not been able to control their descent and had smashed into the wall several times. Fortunately, no one was seriously hurt.

One by one, the guys descended and joined Pal and me. All were safely down. Again, relief swept over me. We high-fived, fist bumped, hugged, and took more group pictures. I was so glad I had waited to share these moments of triumph with my team. My body was chilled from standing in the cold rain, but my heart was warm and content.

The team near the base of the limestone wall, from left: Carol Masheter, Dan Zokaites, Ivan Carrasco, Pal Tande, Denis Verrette, Dave Mauro, Steven Lewi, photo by Raymond Rengkung, July 11, 2012.

We fell into line behind Steven and Dan and tramped back to Base Camp together in the rain. After about half an hour, Steven and Dan said they would go ahead and help get dinner started. When they were out of sight, the rest of us wove through boulders and low ridges of limestone, which blocked our view of Base Camp below. "Are you sure this is the right way?" asked Denis anxiously. "I think so," I said, hoping I was right. Fatigue from a long day of climbing was catching up with us. The last thing we needed now was to get lost in the cold rain. I was relieved, when we climbed the last ridge and could see our tents below on the middle lake's shore.

Back at Base Camp, we were tired, wet, and cold from our long summit day. However, after changing into dry base layers, we enjoyed reliving our successful climb over dinner, a variation on

French toast made from bread dipped in powdered cheese and then fried. It was a strange meal, but it provided calories to heat our chilled, tired bodies. "You were wonderful today," Denis told me in his heavily accented English. "Thanks, Denis, but the climbing and rappelling I can do. It's hiking through the jungle that's difficult for me," I replied awkwardly. I was caught off guard by his compliment, yet my heart glowed with pride, giving me a needed boost to face tomorrow and the challenging days ahead. I suppressed a fleeting fantasy about a helicopter showing up and flying us to Sugapa.

July 12, 2012. As the sun rose, I wished we could rest here in Base Camp for a day. I was tired and achy from our 10 ½ hour summit climb. I dreaded the hard days ahead, of hiking back to Sugapa. However, if we were to return in time for our porters to vote in the special election, we could not take any rest days. In fact, we needed to cover the same difficult terrain in less time than it took us to get here. Though the net elevation change would be lower than where we now stood, we would have to gain and lose several thousands of feet daily over the same formidable, mountainous terrain. My inner whiner moaned. The trip from Sugapa to Base Camp had been very hard. I could not imagine moving fast enough to get back in time for the porters to vote.

Last night's rain had stopped, and the clouds were breaking up, promising a clear morning. After breakfast, we broke camp and headed back over the New Zealand Pass. The hiking seemed easier, and we seemed to go faster today than when we had crossed the Pass from the opposite direction two days ago. However, as though making up for a late start yesterday, today's rain started soon after we left camp and continued most of the day.

Beyond New Zealand Pass, we came to the steep, exposed ledges that we had climbed two days ago. A fall here would be bad. As when we were here before, Dan asked whether anyone wanted to be belayed. No one spoke up. Dan followed Steven down the first ledge and waited near the bottom, holding his umbrella over his head in the rain, and watched me to be sure I got down safely.

Carol Masheter climbing down limestone fins, Dan Zokaites watching, photo by Pal Tande, July 12, 2012.

Right after I had down-climbed the first the ledge, I heard sharp, rapid little gasps behind me, the kind I make, when I am scared. I looked back up the ledge to see who was in trouble. Pal had stopped in a frozen crouch facing the wall. He didn't know where to place his feet. I turned around, climbed back up, and said in what I hoped was a reassuring voice, "There's a good place for your right foot here," and I guided his foot down with my hands to a solid hold, "And here for your left foot," guiding his other foot. We continued this way, until he was safely down from the scary bit. Dan nodded approvingly and encouraged us to help each other like this. It felt good to help one of the guys, especially since they had been so patient and helpful with me.

Peace Fire

July 13, 2012. This morning I awoke to find myself nose to nose with Dan. He opened his eyes slowly, gazed at me with dark-rimmed blue eyes, smiled sleepily, and said, "Good morning." I grinned back, thinking his girlfriend was a very lucky lady and remembering the quiet joy I had experienced years ago, when I awoke next to someone I loved. Then I snapped back to the here and now. I rolled over in my sleeping bag to give him some privacy, while he dressed.

After breakfast and the daily argument between Jemmy and the porters, we left camp and continued crossing the boggy plateau. We stopped for a lunch break just below the top of a low hill with less gooey mud. While I sat pawing listlessly through my food bag, looking for something that would not upset my temperamental gut, some of the guys called, "Come see this." I was tired and almost did not climb to the hill top, where the guys were looking down at something, but curiosity got the better of me. I trudged up to join them. At first a star-burst pattern of half-burned sticks looked like an old camp fire. On closer inspection, I realized the sticks were a circle of half-burned bamboo bows and arrows.

"It's a peace fire," someone said. Our Indonesian guides nodded in agreement. Our best guess was that this was a ritual burning of weapons between warring tribes to end a conflict. I picked up and examined the unburned end of a bow. Like the bows I had seen some of our porters carrying, it was made from split bamboo and was nearly straight. It still had elaborate weaving of thin strands of bamboo to secure a bowstring. Each bow had a different woven pattern and simple, yet elegant, black markings, perhaps indicating the individual who owned the bow. The unburned ends of the arrow shafts also had beautiful markings.

These remnants were exactly the kind of souvenir I wanted to bring home from this climb, something unusual and genuine, not something shoddily made for tourists. However, the half-burned weapons probably had significance to the local people. It was best to leave them where we found them, just as we had left the beautiful bow Ivan had found two days ago on our way up New Zealand Pass. We took only pictures of the burned remnants as our souvenirs.

After lunch, we hiked a few more hours across the plateau, crossing several rivers among sharp ridges of karst. We spotted a column of smoke and a large orange tarp on the edge of one of the clumps of forest sooner than we expected. "Perhaps it's the camp of another climbing expedition rumored to be in the area," I wondered aloud. "No," Dan replied, "our porters have not moved camp several more miles toward Sugapa, as Steven had instructed them. We will have to camp here today." Having a shorter, easier day was nice, but then we would have even less time to get back to Sugapa in time for the porters to vote. *Worrying about it won't help,* I reminded myself. *Best to enjoy this easier day.*

July 14, 2012. Today I tried to convince Dan that I had recovered from my gut troubles and could carry my own climbing pack. He insisted that a porter carry it again today. I filled a one-liter water bottle, stuffed my pockets full of snacks, and reluctantly left my climbing pack with the duffels and other gear for the porters would carry. Dan offered to carry my water bottle, so my hands would be free to use my hiking poles. I tried to accept the help graciously, but as usual I felt like I was not doing my share.

We crossed the boggy plateau and plunged into the jungle, struggled up and down steep forested hills, sank into and fought our way out of knee-deep mud. *Yesterday's shorter hike had been too good to be true,* I grumbled to myself. *Now we all, guides, climbers and porters alike, are paying for it.*

Steven dropped behind, while the rest of us continued. Later Steven told us that one of our women porters had collapsed at a river crossing. We were concerned that she was seriously ill. Dan suggested that she not carry a load today. However, later she and her family caught up with us. She still looked ashen and unwell, but she was carrying a load. *Apparently Papuan women do not get sick days. And unlike me, no one is carrying her load.*

We did not see the porter who was carrying my climbing pack all day. I ran out of water and ate all the snacks I had stuffed into my pockets. By late afternoon, I was dehydrated, faint from low blood sugar, and sore from many hard falls. My irritable bowel symptoms were having a field day without my usual weapons, Citrucel and Gentlelax, to tame their tantrums. Adding insult to injury, a nasty cold that had been working its way through our team had finally caught up with me. My sinuses hurt, and my throat was raw. I felt lousy. Dan mooched water from the other team members for me and poured it into my empty water bottle. I felt like a burden to the group. When Dan asked how everyone was doing, Dave quipped, "I would have liked to have been in camp four hours ago." Chanting Mr. T's mantra to myself, "quit yo jibba jabba," helped me avoid saying something crabby. Dave's humor reminded me that we all were very tired.

We struggled on, hour after hour. During one of our short rest breaks that afternoon, I sat slumped with fatigue. My dim brain registered bits of conversation about Roger's snacks. Roger? Then I remembered, just before Roger left the trip after our first day in the jungle, he had given away his food. I had not taken any, because I already had plenty of my own. However, today my food was somewhere else in the jungle with a porter. Dan handed me a piece of salami from Roger's cache. I normally I don't like salami, but today it tasted wonderful. Pal passed me a piece of his favorite chocolate. These gifts gave me an emotional as well as a physical boost. My gloomy mood lifted, and energy seemed to flow magically into my tired body. Grins split the guys' faces, furred with several days' growth of beard. Their cheer was contagious. I grinned through my fatigue and joined in praise of Roger's and Pal's generous gifts.

After sharing snacks that afternoon, I thought we must surely be close to our next camp. I was wrong. For hours we contoured several large hills in giant arcs, swinging out on the edge of one hill, only to see yet more hills ahead and no sign of camp. I now could see the fatigue in the guys' haggard faces, grimed with sweat and mud. We kept going, beyond complaining or joking, focusing on each step, trying not to slip, trip, or fall. We must have looked like a lost battalion from some forgotten war.

As daylight faded into the shadows of the jungle, we finally saw smoke from what I hoped was the porters' fires. We stumbled wearily for another hour in deepening dusk. At last I could see one of our familiar tarps stretched over a frame of branches and our duffels piled nearby. We were finally in camp. I was too tired to care.

At dinner, Steven's usual serious frown melted. He told us he had never seen a group cover the rugged terrain between Camp 5 and Camp 3, two hard days of walking, in such a short time: 15 miles in 10 1/2 hours. This was high praise, as Steven had led many groups through the jungle. We were back on schedule to get to Sugapa in time for the porters to vote. We beamed at each other, tired and muddy yet very pleased with ourselves.

A Different Kind of Christianity

July 15, 2012. I could hear hymns being sung. *Weird. Are the hymns a drug-induced dream from my malaria prevention medication?* I wondered. *No, I am wide awake lying next to Dan in our tent. There are no churches here in the jungle. Where are the hymns coming from?* The singing continued to rise and fall in stately, three-part harmony. I could not make out the words, but the familiar strains were beautiful, even if they seemed out of place. At breakfast, Jemmy explained that Raymond was conducting Mass for the porters.

Raymond later explained to us that Papuans practiced a different kind of Christianity. For example, some Papuan men had more than one wife, though they considered themselves to be Christians. One reason our porters had passed us nearly every day in the jungle was that they wanted to get to camp early in order to have sex with their wives. As in other parts of the world, Papuans blended some aspects of Christianity, like wearing clothes, attending Mass, and singing Christian hymns, with older traditions, such as tribal warfare and polygamy.

On my way to breakfast, one of our porters, a very dark, short man with a lined face, stood in front of me, pointed at my red bicycling shirt, and looked sad. I guessed he wanted my shirt. I felt bad for him. He had so little, and I had so much. However,

I needed my shirt, at least until the end of this trip. Also, Dan and Steven had advised us not to give things directly to individual porters. Doing so could cause jealousy and fights. We would have opportunities to donate clothing and gear to our porters, after we returned to Sugapa.

After packing up my sleeping bag and pads, I was about to zip my duffel closed, when another porter approached me. He pulled my climbing helmet out of my duffel and tried to put it on my head. As I dodged, he started pulling out one of my jackets. I understood that he wanted me to wear my gear, so he did not have to carry it. I was annoyed. We were back in the hot, humid jungle. The last thing I wanted to do was to wear more clothes. I understood that he wanted to carry less weight. I wanted to carry less weight. After many days in the jungle he was tired, I was tired, we all were tired. However, he was being paid to carry 37 pounds of my stuff for an agreed-upon wage. Apparently, Papuans regarded all agreements as subject to negotiation every morning. I remembered Dan's instructions to refer all matters regarding the porters to Jemmy, our expert in local relations. I waved Jemmy over and explained what was going on. After a loud, arm-waving discussion between Jemmy and the porter, Jemmy nodded to me. I put my stuff back in my duffel, zipped, and locked it. I tried to pat the porter's shoulder as a friendly thank-you. He angrily shrugged away my hand, shouldered my duffel, and strode away.

The incident left me with a bad feeling. Our porters lived difficult lives and were working hard to provide us with much needed help. I asked Jemmy if I could pay extra money to the porters who had been carrying my climbing pack. "They are already being very well paid, Miss Carol," he answered. I asked whether I could buy arrows and a bow or a boar's tusk necklace from any of the porters. "We'll see," Jemmy smiled.

That evening Jemmy presented me with a boar's tusk necklace. He told me that the boar's tusk is a symbol of courage and strength among the Papuans. "How much?" I asked. Jemmy shook his head and smiled. "It's a gift. The porters are very impressed with you. They want to give you a ceremony." As I wrapped the necklace and packed it carefully, I wondered what the ceremony would be like.

July 16, 2012. Today the terrain gradually became less challenging. I remembered how difficult it was that first rainy night, when we left Sugapa in a hurry. However, nearly two weeks of long, strenuous days had taken a toll on my 65-year-old body. I fell often. I was not sure why. Perhaps I had become complacent and over-confident. Maybe I was simply tired from long hard days and night after night of poor sleep. Deep muscle bruises jabbed my gluts, thighs, and calves with every step. Bone bruises on my tail bone, knees, and shins hurt like the devil. I hobbled through the jungle like an arthritic monster, my mud-caked clothes hanging from my body like elephant hide.

I had spoken too soon about this jungle hike getting easier, I thought grumpily. Crossing each of the local stick bridges over rushing rivers brought flashbacks of Dori's terrifying fall. To see better, I took off my sunglasses, which I had been using as eye protection from thorns and branches. I put them in a tough Cordova case, and clipped the case to my belt. Later in the day, I realized that the case was gone, probably ripped away by tough jungle vines. Now I was without eye protection from the intense Equatorial sun. *Worrying about it won't help,* I reminded myself.

Hour after hour we fought our way up slippery, steep slopes. We braced ourselves against trees and rocks to keep from falling down steep gulches. We plunged into mud holes masquerading as solid ground and lunged out of them. At times I thought we were lost in hell.

At other times I felt like we were the true descendants of Adam and Eve wandering through a lost Eden. Jemmy found and shared with us green, egg-sized elephant fruit with a thick skin and mildly sweet pulp. Steven cut and split pieces of wild sugar cane and gave us bits to chew, as we walked. The cane was sweeter than the honeysuckle nectar I had sipped as a child.

We passed one hut, then another, then clusters of huts. We were re-entering areas where people lived. We stopped for a rest break at the guest house in Sunama, where we had stayed our first two nights in the jungle, then continued on. *It can't be long now, I thought, only three hours to where the motorbikers had dropped us off on our way in.*

Local people treated us differently now. They did not stop us and demand payment to cross their lands. Instead, men sitting in front of their huts grinned broadly and gave us the thumbs up sign, as we walked by. *Had word spread that our climb had been successful? I wondered. Were they glad to see their kinsmen home safe? Were they looking forward to a celebration?*

Papuan men welcoming us back near Sunama, photo by Ivan Carrasco, July 16, 2012.

At a cluster of huts further down the trail, Jemmy led us into a court yard of packed earth. Papuan boys were chasing hoops made from strips of bamboo bent and tied into a circle, a game straight out of an earlier time. My head spun at the contrast between such enchanting innocence and the complex layers of conflict in this part of the world. The boys chasing hoops reminded me that people, especially children, will find joy even in the most difficult circumstances.

We stopped and sat in the shade of a local house. Sweating in the Equatorial heat like horses after a hard-run race, the guys took off their shirts. I was tempted to strip to my sports bra, but I had not seen any local women without shirts. I didn't want to offend local sensibilities or draw even more attention to ourselves. Already children peered at us from around the edge of the house, eyes sparkling with curiosity.

Jemmy passed around tangerines he had bought from an old woman sitting in front of her hut as well as more elephant fruit, sugar cane, passion fruit, and white, onion-like things that were crunchy and mildly sweet. We feasted on these local delicacies, until we were sticky with their juice and could eat no more.

Sitting in the shade would not get us to Sugapa. The guys stood up and shouldered their packs. Bloated from eating so much delicious fruit, I got to my feet sluggishly and followed them. We climbed over pig fences, crossed stick bridges, and traversed steep, crumbly hillsides above rushing rivers. My energy level fluctuated wildly. With each familiar sight, excitement surged through my body, and a happy chant sang inside my head, *getting closer, almost there!* I would walk faster and even skip or gallop clumsily down some of the hills in my mud boots. Then fatigue and soreness would catch up with me, and I would stumble, catch myself before I fell, and resume my lumbering walk. I wondered whether we would ever get to Sugapa.

We came to a wide dirt road, where the motorbikers had dropped us off nearly two weeks ago. *Yay!* I cheered inwardly. *The long, weary walk is over!* However, no motorbikes were in sight. Jemmy told us that a motorbike crash resulting in injuries had occurred a few days ago, and the Indonesian police had fined the driver. Now motorbikers were reluctant to carry passengers. My heart fell. We were still miles from Sugapa.

We trudged along the dusty road up and down endless hills. Hours passed. Suddenly three motorbikes appeared on a hill top in front of us. After a brief negotiation, Jemmy waved me toward

one of the bikes, "You go first, Miss Carol." I was more than
ready to ride instead of walk, my decades-ago creepy experience
with a motorbiker who was into bondage, now a faded memory.
I fumbled inside my climbing pack, found my climbing helmet,
and strapped it onto my head. I shouldered my pack and swung
my leg over the bike seat behind the slender Indonesian driver.
Remembering instructions Jason had given us at the start of the
trip, I braced my feet on the passenger foot posts and grabbed the
metal rim at the back of the seat behind me.

The motorbike grumbled uphill through loose gravel and dirt.
At the top of the hill, the engine roared, as the driver accelerated.
What young man doesn't like to go fast? I mused. I was pleasantly
surprised to find that I was not as fearful about crashing or falling
off as during my previous ride. Perhaps now riding a motorbike
seemed relatively safe, after the challenges of the jungle and the
climb we had experienced.

A new concern surfaced. As we entered the town of Sugapa,
I did not recognize anything along the road. I hoped Jemmy had
told the driver to take me to the guest house. I hoped the driver
knew how to get there, because I could not remember the way.
Once we were in town, we zig-zagged through unfamiliar streets
crowded with ramshackle shacks. *None of this looks right. Where
is this guy taking me? There have been recent kidnappings of
foreign visitors here.* Fears of being held for ransom or worse
began to race around inside my head.

My driver stopped. We were in front of the guest house.
Giddy with relief, I dismounted the bike, clapped the driver on his
shoulder, and said, "Thanks for a great ride! You're an excellent
driver!" The young Indonesian ducked his head shyly then took
off. Raymond soon arrived on the back of another motorbike.
Inside the guest house, he gestured toward some six-ounce cans of
carbonated drinks. Thirsty, I opened one and drained it, then went
for a second.

I went in search of a long-anticipated shower. Connected to
the guest house by a rickety board walk, the shower shack was
pretty basic. Inside I found a sliver of soap, a battered metal cup,
a worn basin, and three large, rusty barrels overflowing with water

piped from a nearby stream. In spite of the midday heat, the water was cold. I dipped water from one of the barrels into the basin, stripped, and washed myself in stages: face and hands, then arms and torso, legs, feet, and finally my hair. The cold water made me flinch and gave me an ice-cream headache, but it felt wonderful to shed two weeks of sweat, blood, mud, and stink. I scrubbed my bra, briefs, and socks with the sliver of soap. I put them on wet followed by my muddy shirt and hiking pants, as I had no other clothes with me, and the porters were still coming with our duffels. I padded onto the guest house porch to warm up in the hot sun.

The guys arrived one by one. They energetically compared notes about their motorbike rides. "I made my driver go really fast," one said. "Mine went faster," another answered. I smiled, enjoying their energy. Porters left our duffels in a pile near the guest house porch. Steven advised us to bring them inside the guest house, as theft was common here. Inside I showed the guys the carbonated drinks and the shower. After their showers, Dave and Ivan sat shirtless in their shorts on plastic patio chairs outside the guest house to the amusement of local Papuans who had gathered to stare at us.

Dan told us we could pile anything we wanted to donate to our porters in a corner inside the guest house. Jemmy would coordinate donations to individuals. Porters crowded in the guest house doorway, pointing at which jacket or shirt they wanted. Near the back of the guesthouse I sorted through my gear and clothes. Again, Dan reminded us not to give directly to individual porters but to let Jemmy coordinate donations.

Part of me wanted to give the porters everything I had. Another part of me recognized that impulsive, one-time gifts would not help the porters to better their lives. They needed long-term strategies, such as better health care, more education, marketable goods and services, better roads and other infrastructure to get their products and services to market. That said, Jason had told us at the beginning of this trip that the porters would appreciate any of our clothes, no matter how muddy, torn, or stinky they were. I added to the donation pile the shirt and hiking pants I had worn in the jungle, rain pants, mud boots, three pairs of socks, and my hiking poles. Giving these things did not match the Papuan woman's act of generosity, when she offered cookies that she probably needed more than I, when I was so sick, but I hoped the porters would find my donated items useful.

That evening we feasted on Jemmy's fried chicken. Though it was full of bone splinters from being chopped into chunks Indonesian style, it was excellent. "Better than Kentucky Fried," some of the guys crowed. Jemmy beamed at our lavish praise and big appetites.

In Search of Penis Gourds

July 17, 2012. Today we were scheduled to fly back to Timika. After a night of poor sleep, I awoke feeling stiffer and sorer than ever. I dreaded even the short, uphill walk through the village to the airstrip.

Jemmy had mentioned to me several times during our last days in the jungle that the Papuan porters wanted to give us a ceremony. I had been very curious about what the ceremony would be like. However, our porters had already dispersed, perhaps in a hurry to cast their votes in the special election. I was disappointed that the ceremony did not happen, and I was sad that I had not had a chance to thank the porters properly for their help. However, I was glad we had returned a day earlier than we had promised to give the porters more time to walk to their polling places. Voting had more potential to improve their lives than any ceremony they might have given us.

Our Indonesian guides found motorbikers who were willing to give us rides to the airstrip. Happy and relieved to be spared from hobbling up and over the hill, I dug my climbing helmet out of my duffel and strapped it on. As my driver and I roared up the dirt road, I marveled at how much smoother this ride felt than the one I had taken two weeks ago to the trailhead. Cool, moist, morning air rushed past my face, as we passed Papuans walking along the roadside. One man was decked out in his finest: an elaborate head dress made of leaves and matching leafy armbands, penis gourd, and a modest little flap of white cloth covering his buttocks. Many people waved energetically and flashed wide grins, as we passed. Sooner than I expected, we crested the ridge, made a hard left turn, and cruised down the gravelly hill to the airstrip, the same hill I had struggled up awkwardly in my mud boots the day we had arrived. A small plane was flying low, about to land. It was our plane.

Back in Timika, the Grand Tembaga had no room for us. While Dan was arranging for us to go to another hotel, the manager found me in the lobby and gave me a copy of "Grasberg," a book written by George A. Mealey, who had begun his mining career in the Moab uranium district in the mid 1950's and had risen to be president of the company, then known as Freeport-McMoran Copper & Gold. Eventually the company's mine became known as the Freeport Mine, the huge, ugly pit we had seen on summit day. I had mixed feelings about receiving this gift. I hated what the Mine was doing to the rivers and forest and the Papuans. However, the book was a detailed, carefully written history of the Mine with beautiful photographs and illustrations. I felt deeply honored to receive such a well-crafted book about this part of the world. I hoped I expressed this adequately to the hotel manager.

The Hotel Timika, where Dan and Steven found us rooms, was several steps down in quality from the Grand Tembaga. In my room, I stripped off my dirty clothes, relishing the thought of a proper shower and shampoo followed by clean clothes. Nothing worked. The shower had no water, the toilet did not flush, the lights and ceiling fan would not turn on. After nearly two weeks in the jungle, I was sick of being hot and dirty. I lost it. I swore, stomped around, and hurled my dirty clothes across the room. *Tantrums are not going to solve these problems. I'm behaving like a spoiled tourist,* I reminded myself. I pulled on my dirty clothes and went in search of the hotel manager. He found me another room. Its shower and toilet worked marginally, but not much else did.

The next morning, there was no breakfast buffet. After a long wait, a slender, young Islamic woman wearing a black hair covering brought us hard-boiled eggs, offering them to us as though they were precious jewels. To her, perhaps they were. I felt ashamed of being so used to abundance that I took things like showers that worked and boiled eggs for granted.

The guys wanted to go shopping for penis gourds. I could not imagine what I would do with a penis gourd, but I tagged along hoping to find locally made bows and arrows to buy. Our driver took us to a number of shops. The first shops did not have any penis gourds or bows and arrows nor did the second or third shop. At the fourth shop, the guys found quite an assortment of penis gourds. While they giggled over the variety of styles and lengths, I poked around in a large basket of bows and arrows in a corner of the shop. They all looked hastily made, not like the beautifully crafted weapons I had seen during our jungle hike. I was bored, hot, sweaty, and ready to leave. A small Islamic woman, perhaps the wife of the shopkeeper, seemed to take pity on me. She disappeared into a back room and reappeared with a carefully made grass skirt. For fun, I tried to tie it around my waist, but it would only go around about two-thirds of my body. The woman for whom it had been made must have been very tiny indeed. I looked at the Islamic woman and shook my head ruefully, trying to make a joke about how it did not cover me properly.

The Islamic woman disappeared again into the back room and returned holding a tribal head dress. It took my breath away. It was an elaborate head band featuring a real bird of paradise. The iridescent green head and breast formed the front, chestnut wing epaulets and back feathers wrapped around the sides of the wearer's head, and delicate white tail feathers created a lacy coronet. I handled it reverently, gently stroking the gorgeous feathers. I was moved by their beauty yet terribly sad that a rare bird had been killed to make an article of human adornment.

This head dress was just the sort of souvenir I wanted to bring home from Papua – authentic, unusual, and beautiful. However, I did not want to support the killing of birds of paradise by purchasing something made from one. Before I realized what I was doing, however, I asked the Islamic woman "how much?" I understood her to say 15 USD. When I started to hand her the bills, she corrected me. It was 150 USD. I snapped back to reality. I needed that money to tip our Indonesian guides later tonight. Also, buying a head dress made from a rare bird went against my sense of ethics. I stroked it one last time and returned it to the Islamic woman. I wished I could have at least taken a picture of it, but my camera had stopped working in the jungle. I had to settle for mental images of that unforgettable head dress.

The guys paid for their penis gourds. During the drive back to the hotel, they gleefully showed me their purchases. Their high spirits helped to dispel my mixed feelings about the head dress. "Pal, why did you buy so many?" I asked. "Well, I need one for work, one for home, one for Sunday...." He joked. Then he told us that he planned to give them to friends and colleagues. *With a friend like Pal....What a guy!*

The next few days were a reintroduction to the world of pampered tourists. We flew to Bali and stayed at a resort hotel near the beach. We paddled in the swim pools during the day and ate freshly caught grilled fish on the beach at sunset. It felt odd to lounge around on over-stuffed couches, eating to our heart's content, drowsily watching the sun slip into the sea, as we relived highlights of our trip. I wondered how our Papuan porters were celebrating.

The next day Dan went surfing. Ironically, I had lived in Southern California during the surfing craze of the 1960s, but I had never tried it. I really wanted to take a surfing lesson. However, I was still very stiff and sore from my many falls in the jungle. I reluctantly decided that a massage at the hotel spa and a swim around the pool were more my speed.

Our Carstensz Pyramid experience was coming to an end, as all things do. Our tight-knit group had begun to disperse. We had already said goodbye to Steven, Jemmy, and Raymond, our hard-working, capable Indonesian guides. Denis had left for Quebec. Dave would soon meet his lady, Lin, and spend time with her at a nice resort in another part of Bali. Pal invited us all to visit him in Norway. Ivan offered to lead us through jungles in the Dominican Republic.

It was time to go home. Part of me looked forward to seeing my friends and recovering from the demands of this trip. Another part of me was sad that this crazy adventure with these wonderful guys and our volatile, argumentative, irascible, kind, generous porters was coming to an end. This ambivalence was familiar. I had experienced it repeatedly, as each previous climbing trip neared its end. Familiarity did not make it easier.

Epilogue

I had two homecomings from the Seven Summits. The first was in March, 2012. After I had returned from Timika to Bali, I had been able to find a flight to Sydney, Australia. There, my Australian/New Zealand friend, Christine Jensen Burke, whom I had met climbing Vinson Massif in Antarctica two months previously, and her friend, Candace Hall, pulled off a series of small miracles, so we were able to climb Mount Kosciuszko, the highest peak in Australia. After we summited, I emailed my friend and former colleague, Tom, from Sydney and gave him the go ahead to notify the media that I had become the oldest woman in the world to summit the original Bass list of the Seven Summits.

During my flights home to Salt Lake, I had not been sure what to expect. Only one disinterested reporter had interviewed me, before I had left home. Now would anyone find my achievement newsworthy? To my surprise, reporters from all the local television stations and newspapers, along with several friends, crowded at the base of the stairs to the Salt Lake Airport's baggage claim area.

Trotting down those stairs I experienced a strange flashback to the day I defended my dissertation at the University of Connecticut in Storrs in 1988. That day, I had presented my work to an audience of about 40 people, including reporters from local newspapers. When my advisors emerged from their conference about whether

I had passed and said, "Congratulations, Dr. Masheter," I was confused for a moment. I looked furtively over one shoulder, then the other, for the mysterious "doctor," before I realized it was I. Today I felt much the same. Was I really the world record holder these people had come to congratulate? Welcome-home hugs and reporters gathering to interview me helped to make it seem real. The excitement of the moment distracted me from my disappointment about finishing with Mount Kosciuszko instead of Carstensz Pyramid.

While waiting to talk with me, some of the reporters interviewed others in the welcome-home crowd. Someone told the reporters, "Enough is enough. There are plenty of mountains here." An older woman reporter then asked me, "Don't you resent such ageism?" Of course I was annoyed by the implication that I should stop climbing big mountains, simply because I was in my mid-sixties. I may have replied by saying something about the difference between chronological age and physiological age and that each person needs to make rational decisions about what she can do without putting others at unnecessary risk. At least I hope I said something this reasonable, because it was what I believe and what still guides my choice of the mountains I climb.

In contrast, my second homecoming in July, 2012, was quiet. No friends or reporters met me at the airport. It was ironic, as summiting Carstensz Pyramid had been more challenging and seemingly more newsworthy. However, the quiet homecoming was planned. I had not notified anyone about my return. My friends and the media had already given me a hero's welcomes in March, after I had summited Kosciuszko. I did not want to exploit the generosity of the media and my friends. Besides, I did not miss questions about "what's next," because I did not know the answers. I was processing a complex mixture of emotions about having finally completed both lists of the Seven Summits, a project that had taken 10 years of preparation plus five and a half years to accomplish. Of course I was pleased to have completed both lists and to have set world records.

I knew that records do not last. Someone will break my records, just as all records are eventually broken. I reminded myself, the real reason I climb is for the way it makes me feel: challenged, energized, grateful, often deeply connected with my climbing companions, and filled with wonder and joy.

If I seem to have included many of the unpleasant aspects of this climb of Carstensz Pyramid in this book, my intent has not been to complain, but to share with readers what it was really like – the good, the bad, and the ugly. Unpleasant experiences, even failure, such as the March trip, can be powerful lessons as well as precursors to positive experiences, such as reaching the summit with my eight prince charmings. For me, the unpleasant aspects made the triumphs and joys all the more precious. I wanted to share them with readers in the context in which I experienced them.

In spite of dangers and discomforts my team mates and I experienced, I have many positive memories. I remember the Schmidt family for their spirit of adventure, their curiosity, and friendliness; the brothers' affectionate teasing and support of each other; their mother's quiet strength.

I remember finding the climb on summit day to be easier than the days of walking through the jungle, a pleasant surprise.

I remember finding the peace fire on our way back to Sugapa, giving me hope that Papuans may find a more peaceful way of life.

I remember sharing Roger's and Pal's classy snacks during our longest and most exhausting day of jungle hiking.

I remember the guides' quiet, competent leadership through good times and bad.

I remember the guys' rowdy shopping trip in Timika for penis gourds and the beautiful yet sad head dress made from a bird of paradise.

I remember our happy days of relaxed celebration in Bali after our successful climb.

Some of my most precious memories feature my eight male climbing companions. We truly shared the "brotherhood of the rope." The guys welcomed and encouraged me, when they could have excluded me. They slowed their pace for me during our jungle hike, when they preferred to go faster. They did not complain, when porters carried my climbing pack through the jungle and did not carry theirs. They tried to help me, when my feet slipped on steep, muddy slopes, when I got stuck in deep mud, and when I fell off the trail. They cheered, when I succeeded in hauling myself across the Tyrolean traverse. They stopped short of the summit, so that I could be the first in our group to touch the top, a priceless gift of gallantry. We laughed together, suffered together, and some of us cried together. After meeting these guys and sharing this adventure with them, no one can now convince me that true chivalry is dead.

The guys' many kindnesses were especially precious to me, because they contrast sharply with my experiences as a young woman. My own father, a progressive guy for his day, tried to persuade me to become a secretary instead of a chemist. At UCLA some of my professors tried to prevent me from taking physical chemistry classes, though I was a chemistry major, and the classes were required to complete my degree. As a woman research chemist, sexual harassment, discrimination, and lower pay than my male colleagues received came with the territory. In my relationships I had fallen in love with men who were not committed to me and had left me feeling rejected and ill-used. Years later, climbing Carstensz Pyramid with eight generous, kind, strong men helped to heal longstanding emotional scars. For this, I will always be grateful to my eight mountain bros.

Equally precious are memories of the kindness and generosity of several Papuan men and women. I will not forget the Papuan man who helped me traverse the steep, unstable hillside during our first rainy night of jungle hiking. Nor will I forget the porter who held my hand, as I timidly shuffled across a slick log bridge above a rushing river. I will never forget the Papuan woman who offered me her own food, when I was sick. Our porters gathered wild sugarcane, elephant fruit, and passion fruit from the jungle and presented them to us as gifts from Eden. These acts of kindness reminded me of the kind of person I want to be.

As of this writing, memories of the jungle hike and Carstensz Pyramid climb resurface often. Each time my boots squish along a muddy trail, and I shudder with girlish disgust, I smile and remember the many kinds of mud in the Papuan jungle. As I scramble up Mount Olympus in the Wasatch Mountains, the sparkle of quartz crystals, as they catch the morning sun reminds me of how the "diamonds" of freezing mist captivated me on the summit ridge of Carstensz Pyramid. When I see the light of discovery in the eyes of audience members, as I show pictures and share experiences from this climb, I remember my own sense of discovery.

In Papua I learned to laugh and cry at the same time, to experience the collision of intense joy and sorrow in the same moment. Out of that strange alchemy came many precious gifts. I was reminded that there is no shame in needing help and graciously accepting it. We members of our Carstensz Pyramid team are fiercely competitive people who are used to being in charge. Those characteristics have served us well, making us accomplished and financially resourceful. On this climb, however, we each set aside our egos. We helped each other, complemented each other's strengths and weaknesses, and we summited as a team.

Seventeen years ago, at 50 years of age, I started high altitude mountaineering to haul myself out of a swamp of anger, depression, and stress-related health problems. Gradually, my focus has shifted from personal challenge to being part of something larger than myself. At first, that meant being a better member on each of my teams at work as well as in the mountains. Then it spread to being a better citizen, doing more to support what is good and effective in the world. First, I gave more generous monetary donations to entities that help others. More recently, I have tried to overcome my shyness and give in more personal ways through writing and public speaking. I hope that sharing my mountaineering experiences inspires people to overcome their own challenges, to dream their dream, and find ways to make it happen.

What's next? I think Eleanor Roosevelt said it best, "Yesterday is history, tomorrow is a mystery, and today is a gift; that's why they call it the present."

Appendix

I am not a historian, but I have learned a bit about Carstensz Pyramid's complex story before, during, and after my trips to Papua. Some readers may find this brief summary helpful for understanding some of the unusual challenges of traveling in Papua and climbing Carstensz Pyramid. Several of the landmarks and places, such as Carstensz Pyramid, the Freeport Mine, and Papua, Indonesia, have been known by other names. For this brief summary and throughout the book, I have used the most recent and most commonly used names for simplicity's sake.

Jan Carstensz, a Dutch explorer commissioned by the Dutch East India Company, is credited as being the first European to see Carstensz Pyramid. On a rare, clear day in 1636, he reported seeing a high, snow-clad peak from his ship, as he sailed along the southern coast of a large island north of Australia. The explorer's contemporaries mocked his sighting, because snow so close to the Equator seemed impossible. Then the peak was all but forgotten for centuries.

In the early 1900s, European adventurers were looking for unclimbed peaks outside Europe. The first efforts to climb in what is now known as Papua were led by Dutch explorers, as the area had been colonized by the Dutch. In 1909 Hendrik Albert Lorentz led an expedition of explorers into the rugged, unmapped interior, where they encountered wary indigenous people, tropical diseases, heavy rains, and oppressive heat. The expedition members struggled as far as snowfields flanking several high peaks, but they failed to summit any of them.

In 1936, the Royal Netherlands Geographical Society sponsored a team of climbers. They climbed Ngga Pulu, a glaciated peak which they thought to be the highest in Papua. However, with the rapid shrinking of the region's glaciers, a nearby unclimbed rocky summit was found to be higher. It is now known as Carstensz Pyramid in honor of the first European to have reported seeing it. World War II interrupted further climbing expeditions during the 1930s and 1940s. After the War, climbers focused on being the first to summit peaks in the Himalayas, such as Mount Everest. Again, Carstensz Pyramid was forgotten.

In the early 1960s mountaineers were again looking for unclimbed peaks to "conquer." Interest in Carstensz Pyramid rekindled. In early 1962 New Zealander Philip Temple led a party of climbers several days through the jungle and over a high pass, which he had discovered the previous year. Beyond this pass, now known as New Zealand Pass in Temple's honor, Heinrich Harrer, a famous German climber and explorer, led Temple plus Russell Kippax from Austria and Albert Huizenga from the Netherlands up a steep limestone wall and along a jagged ridge to its highest point, becoming the first people known to stand on the summit of Carstensz Pyramid. A decade later, Reinhold Messner summited by a different route on the East ridge. Since then, several other routes have been pioneered, ranging in difficulty from 5.8 through 5.11 according to the Yosemite rating system.

In recent years the number of Carstensz Pyramid summiters has been difficult to determine. Records of climbers who access the area via the Freeport Mine road or helicopter are often missing. Also, some guide companies and independent climbers may not report whether they summit. However, Jason Edwards, who has guided climbers up Carstensz Pyramid several times, has estimated that during recent periods of relative political calm, a few dozen climbers have summited Carstensz Pyramid each year.

To understand why things can go wrong on a climb of Carstensz Pyramid, a bit of additional background may be useful. Much of Papua is very rugged terrain, some of which has not yet been properly mapped. The few passable roads are near the coasts. Even in recent times access to the interior has been limited to a few dirt airstrips then days of strenuous travel on foot. Much of the interior is steep, thickly forested mountains with churning rivers and knee-deep mud. Daily rains, heavy at times, and tropical diseases, such as malaria, add substantial challenges. Being only a few degrees south of the Equator, Papua's climate is more or less uniform year round: hot, humid, and rainy in the jungle; windy with freezing mist, rain, ice, and snow in the high mountains.

For generations, Papua has been populated by tribes that outsiders have described as living in the Stone Age. Papuans have traditionally survived by gathering wild fruits and greens from the jungle, fishing, and hunting wild boar, birds, and any other animals they could catch or shoot. More recently, they have supplemented wild foods by growing yams, domesticated pigs, and chickens on terraces they have built on steep hillsides. The rugged terrain has isolated tribes from each other, resulting in approximately 250 languages. Papuans living in adjacent valleys may not speak each other's language. Different tribes may regard each other as enemies and even as not human.

For centuries tribal warfare has been a big part of Papuan life. Warriors still kill members of enemy tribes with poison-tipped arrows, machetes, and, when they can get them, guns. According to long-standing tradition, if one tribe kills 20 members of another tribe, the second tribe is obliged to kill 20 members of the first tribe. Warriors target women, children, and elderly people as well as men of fighting age.

Papua also has a complex political history. During World War II the eastern part of the island was occupied by Germans, who were eventually defeated by Australians. After World War II, this part of the island became an independent country known as Papua New Guinea. Indonesia took over control of the western part of the island from the Dutch in the 1960's with the support of the United States to keep Indonesia on the American side during the

Cold War. Now called Papua, Indonesia, the transition of power was far from peaceful, as many Papuans expected independence similar to that of the eastern half of the island.

In the late 1960s, a plebiscite took place, as specified by the United Nations. A thousand hand-picked representatives voted on the question of independence for the people of Papua. The results favored continued Indonesian rule. However, those in favor of independence questioned whether the representatives really reflected the will of the majority. Critics claimed that the representatives had been coerced into voting for continued Indonesian rule.

Since then, various groups of Papuans have continued to protest Indonesian rule. Some have engaged in peaceful demonstrations, such as marches and independence-flag-raising ceremonies. Armed separatist militias have made sporadic armed attacks on those perceived to be in power. The local Indonesian military and police have responded by harshly suppressing peaceful as well as non-peaceful protests. Papuans have retaliated, sometimes killing a few Indonesians, who in turn killed a larger number of Papuans, fueling further protests and conflict. Foreign workers and visitors have sometimes been caught up in these conflicts and have been kidnapped, injured, or killed. From 1996 through 2005 the Indonesian government responded to outbursts of violence by closing the Carstensz Pyramid region to outsiders, including mountaineers.

More recently, the United Nations pressured the Indonesian government to hold special elections in which Papuans have voted for increased autonomy. However, the Indonesian government's version of increased autonomy has fostered erratic frontier justice meted out by local Indonesian military and police officers. Though journalism has been heavily restricted, several reports of human rights violations by Indonesians against Papuans have been made public.

Foreign extraction of Papua's rich resources has also fueled conflict. First Dutch and then American geologists discovered rich deposits of copper and gold near Carstensz Pyramid. Before World War II, the area was considered to be inaccessible; the tantalizing metals might as well have been on the moon. However, after transfer of control of the region from the Dutch to the Indonesians in the 1960s, foreign companies began to develop mines and create access to them. A U.S. mining company, as of this writing known as Freeport, spent three years opening a huge, open-pit mine. To access the mine, Freeport built a road through 63 miles of nearly impassible terrain. Freeport also built a 68-mile long slurry pipeline to transport ore from the mine at 12,000 feet elevation to an ore mill at 10,000 feet elevation. From its perspective, Freeport has invested heavily in infrastructure to access Papua's rich resources and has felt entitled to large profits.

The years since 2000 have been especially marred by violence and negative publicity. Many Papuans have felt that they have not benefited from the Freeport Mine's vast wealth. In fact many Papuans have experienced harm from Freeport's activities. Toxic effluent from the Mine has killed fish and devastated forest, upon which many Papuans have traditionally depended to feed their families. Reporters made public the devastation of over eleven square miles of rain forest and pollution of the river system near the Freeport Mine caused by toxic waste rock.

Reporters also uncovered Freeport's payment of over 20 million U.S. dollars from 1998 through 2004 to secure the ore reserves by paying off Indonesia's dictator, his cronies, local military commanders, and local police. Today, many Papuans resent anyone that they believe to be associated with the Freeport Mine, particularly Americans. Other countries have distanced themselves from the Freeport Mine. Following recommendations from ethics councils, Norway, New Zealand, and Sweden have excluded Freeport stock from investment portfolios for their national pension funds.

In October, 2011, 70 percent of Freeport Mine workers joined a strike, demanding higher pay. Strikers blocked the road and cut the slurry pipeline in several places. Freeport halted its operations amid deteriorating security and intensified demonstrations for Papuan independence. Reports of Indonesian security forces beating and killing peaceful Papuan demonstrators hit the news. The Indonesian government again closed the area to outsiders, including those who wanted to climb Carstensz Pyramid, until the explosive situation simmered down.

In early 2012 the area around Carstensz Pyramid was reopened to outsiders, but it was far from safe. Armed guards escorted shifts of workers to and from the Freeport Mine to protect them from attacks. Papuans have tended to assume that people with light complexions, including foreign climbers, were associated with the Freeport Mine or the Indonesian rulers, making them a target for resentment and occasionally violence.

Racism and religious differences have also contributed to conflict in Papua. Some Europeans, Indonesians, and others have regarded the Papuans as "primitive" and "inferior." Even in recent times, people in power are rumored to have hunted and killed Papuans, as though they were animals. Since the 1960s missionaries have converted many Papuans to Christianity. Most Indonesians, who live and work in Papua, are Islamic. These religious differences sometimes contribute to conflicts between Indonesians and Papuans.

Three weeks after I returned home from summiting Carstensz Pyramid, I learned that four friends I had met on previous climbs had been kidnapped by armed men. My friends were members of the Adventure Consultants Carstensz Pyramid Expedition in August 2012 that I had tried to join, but the trip had been full.

The expedition members had flown from Timika to Ilaga. All seemed to have begun well. They had started hiking from Ilaga toward Base Camp, when only hours later, a Papuan separatist militia stopped them. The men claimed to be against the Indonesian government. These men forced the expedition members into a small hut, confiscated their passports, and set fire to the area surrounding the hut, so no one could escape. The armed men demanded 110,000 USD, which the expedition members did not have. After hours of tense negotiations, the militia accepted 3,500 USD in exchange for the expedition's immediate departure from Papua. The ordeal was over. No one was hurt, but several expedition members were very shaken, and needless to say, they were forced to leave without having a chance to climb Carstensz Pyramid.

I was stunned, when I heard this news. Had that expedition not been full, I would have been a member of it and would have been kidnapped as well. I had heard about such dangers before my own climb, but a part of me naively did not believe anything like that would happen to me or people that I knew. Through dumb luck I had dodged a bullet. I was very relieved that my friends and the other expedition members were safe, but I could only imagine their fear and confusion, while they were held captive.

I was reminded that Papua is still an unpredictable, dangerous place not only for the people who live there but also for those who come to climb Carstensz Pyramid. In addition to the many cross currents of violence, bribery and corruption within the entities that issue permits to climb Carstensz Pyramid make gaining legal access to the area unreliable. Those interested in this climb would be wise to go with a mountaineering company that knows how to obtain legitimate access to the mountain and how to deal with local authorities and tribal groups. In addition to careful preparation and fitness training, a bit of luck helps.

CPSIA information can be obtained
at www.ICGtesting.com
Printed in the USA
FSHW020902200320
68296FS